Singleness for Struggling Romantics

SINGLENESS
for struggling romantics

Daniel Carpenter

Cover design by Jesse Grimm

ISBN 979-8-9946726-0-0 (paperback)
ISBN 979-8-9946726-1-7 (ebook)

*To my future wife, whom
I am waiting and praying for.*

*To Mom and Dad, who love me
regardless of my marital status.
I hope to have as loving and as durable
a marriage as yours someday.*

*To Josh, my beloved brother, who died
while these pages were still being written.
Of all the supportive voices for this work,
I lament that I cannot hear yours.*

*To God, the Author of my life,
whose pen strokes I can never predict.
Though my struggles may be great,
your love is greater still.*

CONTENTS

INTRODUCTION

I've been a romantic for as long as I've had hormones. My earliest memory of this was back in middle school where I was lying in bed, praying about godly things. You know, stuff like getting a girlfriend. I couldn't fall asleep because my desire for a relationship was so intense. I found women both beautiful and fascinating. They were so similar to me and yet so different, and those differences enticed me. The idea of being wanted by one of them—not just physically, but emotionally and mentally and spiritually—sounded every bit like a "happily ever after".

But what if I found a girlfriend tomorrow, and then she broke up with me that same day? Technically, my prayer would be answered. As I wrestled with this, the true nature of my desire became clear. I was looking for someone who didn't just want me but was committed to me and would stay by my side no matter what. And so, I changed my prayer. Instead of a girlfriend, I began praying for God to give me a wife.

He didn't answer my prayer in middle school, but I wasn't too worried—I still had time. As I entered high school, I wondered if I would find my future wife there. After all, I had heard plenty of stories about high school sweethearts—

perhaps that would happen to me. As each year passed, I was on high alert. I looked for my future wife at school. I looked for her at church. If she was attractive, appeared to love Jesus, and breathed the same air that I did, she was a possibility.

I wasn't the only one looking for love. One by one, my friends started dating. I watched, aghast, as each relationship crashed and burned. Once filled with dreams of love, they soon became rife with nasty breakups, poor communication, and broken hearts. As I watched these tragedies unfold, I realized my desire for marriage was missing a few vital steps. In order to have a quality marriage, I needed a quality woman. In order to attract a quality woman, I needed to be a quality man.

How exactly does one become a quality man? During my sophomore year, I went on the hunt for answers. I scoured the internet and the local library for Christian podcasts, books, and articles on all things dating and marriage . . . and sometimes singleness, although the idea of staying single made me feel uneasy. The only thing I was focused on was being the best godly husband possible so I could have the best godly marriage possible.

This "learning spree" taught me much. Not only did I grow in my knowledge and understanding of biblical love, I was already devoting most of my own thoughts to the topic. Sometimes, a few of my friends would ask me for dating and relationship advice. Apparently, I knew a lot for someone my age.

Time passed. I had graduated and was now going to college. Relationships continued to happen around me, but this time—instead of ending in breakups—many of them ended in marriages. One by one, my friends found spouses. After just a few years, it seemed as though singles were now an endangered species.

Due to my know-how in all things biblical and marital, peers came to me for guidance. I found myself having conversations with couples and the few singles still in existence. While it was an honor to be trusted by so many, it often felt like I was cursed. I was helping others with their love lives, but nothing was happening in mine. I would go on dates and get into relationships, but nothing seemed to last. Several women found their spouses a month or two after dating me. Most singles I befriended found relationships, married, and were never heard from again. It felt like everyone had the golden ticket to Willy Wonka's chocolate factory except me. I felt like I was falling behind in life. "Happily ever after" felt further and further away.

For the first time in my pubescent life, I had to confront the singleness that I had long been avoiding. The very idea of this made me uncomfortable, as I had always feared that my singleness was actually a life sentence. I wanted a way out. I wanted results, and yet, the lack of results spoke louder. Seeing this tension within me, friends and strangers alike would attempt to offer me their "thoughtful" advice.

"Have you given it to the Lord?"

"It's okay, you'll find someone . . ."

"Maybe God is keeping you single for a reason . . ."

Maybe you should shut up, Tiffany.[1]

I ended up graduating college unmarried and confused. I had done everything I could think of doing: I had tried being a "good Christian" by staying patient and content. I had dated with healthy boundaries and treated women with respect. I had been a counselor for a Christian summer camp and gone to a Christian college—institutions known as petri dishes for marriages-to-be. I was passionate about my faith, passionate about marriage, and had (I'm told) a winning personality. I checked every box. And yet, no matter what I did "right", and no matter how many times I "should" have found a wife, I still remained single.

The years after college were full of change. I moved from one state to another. I lived in cities, suburbs, and even a farm at one point. I was involved in churches both as a volunteer and as a full-time staff member. I led small groups for singles. I was part of small groups where I was the *only* single.

Throughout these different contexts, my perspective began to mature. I realized that while my desire for marriage was good, I had made it into an idol. I had dedicated most of my thoughts and ambitions to marital love, treating my faith as a tool to help me obtain it. The "happily ever after" I had been chasing was a spouse instead of God. While my love for Jesus was a big part of my life, my love for marriage was greater.

I began to see that there were opportunities my singleness had that—because of my obsessive focus on marriage—I hadn't noticed before. I was growing deeper in my faith and loving others in ways that wouldn't have happened the same way if I had been married. Even in my struggles and frustrations, I saw God at work. Just because I desired marriage didn't mean I should ignore the blessings and benefits of my singleness.

These discoveries were good, but now I had to reconcile my desire for marriage with the reality of my prolonged singleness. If I continued to see marriage as a source of ultimate fulfillment, I would be neglecting my relationship with God. At the same time, it would be impossible for me to ignore my romantic desires since I still wanted a wife someday. I couldn't continue to be a marriage-worshipping romantic nor pretend to be a struggle-free single. Instead, I had to learn to live faithfully as a struggling romantic.

• • •

Throughout my single years, despite how much I knew about scripture and despite everything I did "right", I was still prioritizing marriage above Jesus. I was giving Jesus my mind, but I was giving marriage my heart. Now, as I've been working on giving all of myself to Jesus, I've begun to see how truly transformational a relationship with him is.

God didn't give us hope in the form of religious beliefs, he gave it to us in the form of a person. If we want to know who God is, we have to enter into a relationship with Jesus. Theological understanding and good behavior are not enough on their own merits.

This is my ultimate hope as you read this book: not just to grow in your knowledge of scripture, but to draw nearer to the person of Jesus. My own understanding is insufficient: I am a flawed human being in the process of being redeemed and restored. But Jesus is more than sufficient—he is everything. He is both the means and the end. He is not only the "happily ever after" we desire, he points us to how we can join him in that "happily ever after" as well. He is both the meaning of life as well as the way to find it. In him, we can thrive in sadness and in joy, in struggles and in success, in marriage and in singleness.

If we don't have Jesus as our primary focus, other desires will compete to take his place in our hearts and we will encounter conflicting messages. Some will say "get married as soon as possible," while others will say, "forget marriage—your career is more important." Some will say "sex is no big deal: it's just biology," while others will warn, "sex is everything and if you screw it up, there's no hope for you." But if you are in Christ, then what he says supersedes all else. He is the anchor which grounds us in the midst of turbulent waters. We must give him space to cut through the noise. We must surrender to him his rightful authority over our lives.

To get our bearings, we need to know where we are and where we might be headed. First, we must understand what Jesus and scripture have to say about singleness and marriage. Singleness is a gift—it is a good thing—as is marriage, although we can distort marriage and see it as something that it actually isn't. We must see both of them the way Jesus did.

Then, we need to apply that same perspective to our present situation as struggling romantics. How does one date as a Christian? What can we do when we feel lonely or unattractive? The Bible may have more to say on these struggles than you might think.

My goal with this book isn't to make you fear or hate marriage. It's to make you to give a crap about your singleness—not seeing it as something to escape but an opportunity to cherish. Life as a struggling romantic is not chiefly about seeking marriage, it's chiefly about seeking Jesus. I want to equip you with tools so you can find hope in him, no matter what your marital status ends up being.

I am still unmarried. I write about the single life because I live the single life each and every day. I'm in the trenches with you; there are times I feel agonizing loneliness and deep longing. Despite all of that, I would not trade these years for anything else. I am grateful for what God has given me, and I want that for your singleness too, whether it lasts for the rest of today or the rest of your life.

PART 1

UNDERSTANDING SINGLENESS & MARRIAGE

1

MORE THAN A LABEL

Here's some friendly advice: if you only know a few basic words of Spanish, don't become a translator.

It all started at a church my family and I used to attend. Once a week, we would volunteer at a ministry there, bagging groceries and handing them out to people in need. In addition to food and clothing, the ministry also offered services to financially struggling families including legal consultations.

I was learning Spanish in high school, and although I only knew a handful of words, the ministry gave me a pin to wear which said "Hablo Español" in bold letters. I didn't think much of it, except as a way to show off that I knew Spanish. Maybe some of the ladies would notice and think of me as "multifaceted".

One day, I was chatting with a few other volunteers when one of our supervisors rounded the corner, worry on her face. She explained that a Mexican family had just arrived for an appointment with one of the lawyers. "Do any of you speak Spanish? I need someone to translate."

I froze. Despite being a teenager, I knew my limits. My Spanish was nowhere near ready for such an undertaking, unless this family wanted me to help them count to ten or ask where the bathroom was. Perhaps, if I slowly moved toward the exit door, the supervisor wouldn't smell my fear.

Then, one of the volunteers spoke up. "Daniel, you speak Spanish, right?"

I felt like Caesar being stabbed by his fellow senators. I thought about bringing up my lack of experience in, well, *anything* Spanish. But then I became painfully aware of the "Hablo Español" pin on my chest, gleaming in the light.

I sighed. "Uh, well, yeah. A little."

"Perfect," she said, waving for me to follow her.

We began walking toward the offices. A lump of dread formed in my throat. I was on a collision course with a family who couldn't understand me and a mountain of expectations I was completely unprepared to fill.

Much like my "Hablo Español" pin, many of us don't see singleness as much more than a label. We may try to hide it, like I wanted to when my supervisor asked for a Spanish speaker, because it feels like a mark of failure or an indicator we're not lovable enough. On the other hand, we can also use our singleness as a justification for doing whatever we want or an advertisement to indicate we're available.

But there's a problem when this happens. I saw this with a guy who attended one of my singles groups. He had spent most of his life dating one person after another. Like Tarzan swinging from one vine to the next, one relationship would end and another would begin shortly after. He had been in so many relationships that he could pinpoint when certain life events had happened based on who he was dating at the time. Because he hadn't thought of singleness as anything more than a label, he hadn't given himself the time to really understand it. As a result, whenever a relationship ended, he felt confused and helpless until the next one came along.

There's far more to singleness than just the label. Like me and my non-existent Spanish, we often don't realize how unprepared we really are until reality strikes. A marriage we were excited for ends, an engagement is suddenly called off, a relationship falls apart, and we find ourselves alone and unsure what next step to take.

Perhaps you've been going from one failed relationship to another and feel a quiet despair as your search keeps coming up empty. Perhaps you want to grow in your relationship with God while single, but you're unsure what to do next. Perhaps something unexpected happened with your significant other, or even your spouse, and you find yourself single again, realizing you've never given singleness much thought. In instances like these, we find ourselves wrapped up in something we aren't ready for.

THE DILEMMA OF SINGLENESS

Singleness, as the Bible defines it, is not that complicated. Are you not married? Are you abstaining from sex? Then you're practicing Christian singleness. Simple, right? However, these practices put us at odds with both western culture and the mainstream American church. As pastor Sam Allberry observes, our secular culture supports being unmarried but dismisses sexual abstinence.[1] Western church culture, broadly speaking, emphasizes sexual abstinence yet tends to see those who are unmarried as second-rate.

Because of this, being a single Christian can feel like being the rope in a tug of war game. On one side, our secular culture has made the benefits of marriage accessible to singles. You can enjoy sex, live with your significant other, and raise children all without ever saying your wedding vows. Marriage, by comparison, looks archaic. Desiring it is treated like going vegan: you can restrict yourself if you want to, just don't impose it on others. Staying single is seen as more freeing and, consequently, is becoming more widely embraced and encouraged. One billboard I saw advertised one-person phone plans with the slogan "another reason to stay single."

In most churches, singles have the opposite problem. They awkwardly stick out in congregations that typically target married couples and young families. Allberry points out that "many of our default settings see singleness in terms of deficiency . . . Single people are *unmarried*, while we would never think of married people as *unsingle*."[2]

When I worked in ministry, I saw this play out in the opportunities churches offered. For the marrieds there were marriage conferences, couples-only small groups, sermons about dating and marriage, mentor couples, marriage ministries, children's ministries, church "date nights", parent conferences, Mother's Day and Father's Day services, and church staff composed almost entirely of married people. Singles, on the other hand, were usually encouraged to serve in student ministries. If the church was big enough, it might have a young adults group they could join. A ministry dedicated entirely to singles is a rare find. While singles aren't explicitly shunned from churches, the lack of outreach can make it feel like there isn't much room for them. As a result, they can wrongly see the church as anti-single.

Between secular culture and this misunderstanding of church culture, we receive mixed messages. One side says being married is a restraint; the other insists it's a requirement for a fulfilling life. One says singleness is the cure, while the other insists marriage is. Between both of these extremes, it can feel like something is inherently wrong with our singleness.

As a result, it's easy to cave into compromise. Some singles stop caring about their faith and embrace the sexual ethic of our culture. Others remain in the church but treat their own singleness with disdain, perceiving it as an affliction. Either way, both of these attitudes deviate from the biblical framework God created, distorting singleness to better fit their respective contexts. So, if both of these misconceptions miss the mark on singleness, how can we deal with this tension?

While many are tempted to label singleness as something to loathe or something to idealize, scripture offers us a third view that elevates singleness beyond just a label. The Apostle Paul, himself a single man, unpacks this:

> Now as a concession, not a command, I say this. I wish that all were as I myself am. But each has his own gift from God, one of one kind and one of another. To the unmarried and the widows I say that it is good for them to remain single, as I am.

(1 Cor. 7:6-8)

What Paul says here was radically countercultural at the time. Getting married and raising a family was everything in Jewish culture: children weren't just an assurance your bloodline would continue; they would work in the family business and help generate income. As you got older and less able to take care of yourself, your children would assist you, since independent living and nursing homes didn't exist. As sources of income, generational legacy, and elder care, marriage and children were essential. Paul's words went against the entire ancient world. No other society or religion thought that remaining single was a legitimate choice anyone could make. Here, however, singleness is far more than just legitimized: Paul calls it a "gift from God". This means that while marriage is desirable, beautiful, and part of God's design, those without spouses can still bring him glory.

THE GIFT OF SINGLENESS

What in the world does Paul mean by singleness being a gift? When Paul advocates for singleness, he points out specific freedoms it brings in comparison to marriage.

> I want you to be free from anxieties. The unmarried man is
> anxious about the things of the Lord, how to please the
> Lord. But the married man is anxious about worldly things,
> how to please his wife, and his interests are divided. And
> the unmarried or betrothed woman is anxious about the
> things of the Lord, how to be holy in body and spirit. But
> the married woman is anxious about worldly things, how to
> please her husband.

> (1 Cor. 7:32-34)

Paul isn't gatekeeping marriage here—he's clarifying it. Singleness and marriage are both gifts from God, each with their own struggles and blessings. For instance, singleness provides a degree of freedom and flexibility that marriage cannot. On a small scale, I've experienced this while making last-minute plans with my friends. If they don't already have something scheduled, those who are single will often say "yes", while I will usually hear from my married friends, "hold on, let me double check with my spouse."

Paul explains that those who are married will have anxieties about "worldly things". This is not a sin. Paul isn't saying these concerns make marriage inferior, he's pointing out they will naturally arise. Between a husband and a wife, there is a necessary care and concern for the other woven into the design of marriage. They have made a sacred, lifelong covenant with one another. You will have more distractions in marriage. In fact, you *should*. If one spouse was completely indifferent to the other's needs, that would be concerning and unhealthy. Those who are married can still maintain a deep relationship with God, but their focus is divided, so it is more difficult.

Singles, on the other hand, are "anxious about the things of the Lord". This is important for us as struggling romantics to consider. If we aren't anxious about God, something else will readily take his place. Just because we have the ability to focus on the things of the Lord doesn't mean it will be easy. We can spend our time chasing career success and playing video games instead. But these are meant to be *parts* of life, not the *purpose* of it. Our foremost concern needs to be on the things of God. Australian preacher John Chapman, who was single his entire life, remarks on how this freedom enhanced his ability to minister:

> I don't think I ever consciously made a decision to stay
> single. I was just too busy with ministry and so didn't get
> around to it. But that is part of Paul's point: singles can be

busy with ministry. They are not distracted with the troubles of the world. Without me ever stopping to think about it, God has given me the gift of singleness.[3]

If you're currently single, the gift of singleness and all the blessings that come with it are readily available for you. There are struggles you will still face, of course, but with them comes an opportunity to secure a passion for Jesus without distraction or competition.

Right now, we are under no lifelong vows. There is no spouse for us to worry about and (for some) no children to provide for. We can wholeheartedly direct our time, abilities, and resources toward God. Marriage isn't meaningless—far from it—but neither is our singleness.

THE GIFT-GIVER OF SINGLENESS

One Christmas, when my brother and I were little, there was a mix-up. We were at our grandparents' house, and when was time to open our presents, they handed us each a large gift. Almost immediately, we began ripping them open.

I could tell that it was a Lego set. But as the wrapping paper fell away, my excitement turned into confusion. It wasn't the Lego set I wanted, not even close. It suited my brother's tastes more than it did mine. Then, I looked over to see what my brother had received: it was the same Lego set I had wished for! Apparently, in the midst of wrapping presents, our grandparents had accidentally switched the Lego sets.

Sometimes, singleness feels like a gift that was given to you but intended for someone else. The friends around you are either married or in relationships. It seems as though everyone else has their love lives figured out, and you feel you've fallen behind. We should joyfully receive singleness as a godly gift, and yet, many of us feel confusion instead. *Did God make a mistake? Have I fallen through the cracks?* Some of you might think, *I still deeply desire marriage, so maybe the gift of singleness doesn't apply to me after all.*

However, unlike my grandparents, God does not make mistakes. If we want to better understand the nature of singleness, we need to better understand the character of God.

God isn't the fast-food worker who messes up your order because he wasn't paying attention to what you were saying. He isn't some trickster who gives gag gifts just to mess with you. God is a divine craftsman who personally fashions his creation. Every detail is deliberately made with care and precision. He made your singleness to bless you, not to hurt you. Nothing God gives us is flawed or evil, for "every good gift and every perfect gift is from above, coming down from the Father of lights" (James 1:17). God is a good and personal God who gives good and personal gifts.

Singleness isn't the only gift from God. Marriage (Prov. 18:22, 19:14) and salvation through Jesus (Rom. 6:23, Eph. 2:8) are gifts from him as well. They are good gifts because they are based on *God's* goodness, not the goodness of our experiences with them. There are unhappy married people just as there are unhappy single people, but the existence of struggle doesn't indicate the absence of the gift. As pastor Timothy Keller asserts, "the 'single calling' Paul speaks of is neither a condition without any struggle nor on the other hand an experience of misery. It is fruitfulness in life and ministry *through* the single state."[4]

Throughout the Bible, we see many men and women experience this fruitfulness as singles. The Apostle Paul was single, and so was Jesus—a perfect human being. God took Joseph from a slave to the second most-powerful man in Egypt before he found a wife (Gen. 41:45). Anna was a widow when she prophesied over a young Jesus (Luke 2:36-38). The prophet Jeremiah was commanded by God to remain single (Jer. 16:1-2). There's no mention of Daniel having a wife, either. The gift of singleness isn't reserved for the "ultra-religious" or for lifelong celibates: it has been given to produce fruitfulness in your single years, however long they may last.

THE FREEDOM OF SINGLENESS

When we question whether we have the gift of singleness, what we usually mean is "does biblical singleness work for me?" We then conclude that if we feel it doesn't work for us, then it doesn't apply to us. But this mindset comes from fixating on the deficiencies of our singleness and ignoring the blessings. If we reject the gift of singleness, we reject what God has given to sustain us in this period away from marriage. If you are currently single, you have been offered the gift of singleness.

Jesus reassures us, "If you then, who are evil, know how to give good gifts to your children, how much more will your Father who is in heaven give good things to those who ask him!" (Matt. 7:11). Whether single or married, we need to prioritize our relationship with the gift-giver above our relationship with the gift.

There's a freedom when this happens. The stress of "figuring out" our singleness and our love life falls away. Just as God gave us the gift of singleness, he's the only one who can give the gift of marriage. Therefore, the burden of finding a wife or a husband does not ultimately rest on our shoulders. God gives us gifts in his timing and at his discretion, not ours. We are not missing out on what God has for us because what he has for us in this moment is singleness.

Make no mistake, there will be struggles in your singleness. At times, you will feel out-of-place in your church or your workplace or even your friend group. Why? Because what God has in mind for your singleness doesn't quite fit what society or mainstream church culture has to say about it, and that's okay. Being "biblically single" doesn't necessarily mean we're content being single, it means we're content being in relationship with God.

Singleness is a gift. Not just a label. Not a consequence of being unattractive or a sign that you're "undatable". Not a punishment or a curse. It's a good gift, a blessing from God himself, therefore the implication is not for us to merely accept it but to delight in it. Singleness is a good thing that has been deliberately formed and purposefully given for your benefit to draw you nearer to your Creator.

Reflection Questions:

• Before reading this book, how would you have labeled your singleness? How have other people labeled your singleness?

• As singles, we encounter conflicting expectations from church culture and secular culture. Do you agree with this statement? In which environment do you struggle the most to feel accepted as a single? In what ways have you felt pressured?

• What thoughts or feelings come to mind when you think of singleness as a gift and God as the gift-giver?

2

THE BIGGEST LIES SINGLES BELIEVE

It's a strange feeling when you go to the concert of a super popular artist you've never heard before.

My friends made plans to see a big-name musician perform live and invited me to go. I hesitated, but they offered to pay for my ticket. How could I refuse? We drove for several hours, found parking, walked to the venue, and waited in the back of a line that wrapped around the entire city block. Apparently, this artist was a big deal: *millions* of people knew his music by heart.

Except for me.

Finally, the line started moving, and we made it inside. I found myself surrounded by thousands of devoted fans. I looked around the cavernous room: most of the people there were teenagers or college students and were wearing the artist's merchandise. I was one of the few men in that room. My friends were chatting among themselves, excited to be there and discussing their favorite songs. I was definitely the odd one out.

The artist and his band walked out onstage. People cheered, and he started performing. Every time the bass rumbled, my organs were rearranged. Some people were listening intently, but others seemed indifferent, which struck me as strange. If they loved this guy so much, why weren't they enjoying the music?

After an hour or so, the band wrapped things up. The artist thanked us and walked offstage. There was some applause. I was confused. Were concerts usually this short?

Then, the emcee walked out and began hyping us up. It finally dawned on me: that had been the *opening act*, not the artist we had come all this way to see! Because I wasn't a devoted fan, I had mistaken the real thing for something else.

In a similar way, we can confuse the gift of singleness God has for us with something else, devoting ourselves to a lie instead of the genuine thing, without being fully aware that's what we're doing.

Devotion is crucial in understanding singleness. In fact, the Apostle Paul explains that singleness exists "not to lay any restraint upon you, but to promote good order and to secure your undivided devotion to the Lord" (1 Cor. 7:35). It's important that we remember Paul's words here, as they form the backbone for this chapter. Singleness isn't aimless; it's purposefully crafted by God so we can secure a devotion to him.

What does Paul mean by "devotion"? When we are devoted to something, we love it consistently and voluntarily. We care about our connection to it. By describing a "devotion to the Lord", Paul is saying we must be "single-minded" in our faith. It's not about neglecting our other relationships but about prioritizing the one relationship that matters most. We do this by establishing good order, maintaining an undivided focus, and ensuring our devotion is to God and God alone.

Three main lies often lead us away from each of these statements: the lies of overindulgence, preoccupation, and evasion. These are traps we fall into that can divert or distort our devotion. Just like I mistook the opening act for the main artist, a lack of understanding can cause us to mistake these lies for the real thing.

These false beliefs bring us into conflict with the created intent behind our singleness, pulling us toward a vacuous life instead of a fulfilling one. Consciously or unconsciously, they come between us and God. By exposing these three false devotions, we can more deeply understand the true devotion our singleness is meant to establish. And the more we cultivate true devotion to God, the less vulnerable we will be to imposters.

THE LIE OF OVERINDULGENCE

"Singleness exists for my benefit."

Singleness offers more freedom than marriage—no one has to hold us accountable if we decide to change our plans, stay out late, spend all our money, or work long hours—but in the face of all this freedom we can take advantage of these opportunities to prioritize *our* glory instead of God's. The unprecedented amount of freedom we enjoy can easily lead to a life of overindulgence, one consumed by distractions and self-gratification.

At the core of this is an avoidance of responsibility. We push aside considerations about marriage, about self-control, and even about faith on the basis that we'll figure it all out when we're older. It becomes all about enjoying our single years while they last. In the grip of this lie, marriage can be seen as inhibiting, as a restriction on one's freedom and happiness, while singleness is seen as self-actualizing, the best and only way to get "in touch" with who you truly are. This is then used as an excuse to self-indulge.

This might look like spending hours on social media or video games, binge-watching shows, working long hours to advance in the career you want, obsessively improving or maintaining your appearance, and so on. More extreme distractions include making extravagant purchases on a regular basis, consuming pornography, eating your feelings, partying the night away, or experimenting with substances and lifestyles that don't align with scripture.

Mind you, these are symptoms, not the main issue. It's fine to go to a party or eat out. It's okay to have fun and enjoy your single years. But there comes a point when you're partying or eating out to maintain your own happiness. This can take many forms, but at its root, overindulgence is a way to avoid taking responsibility for your life.

There's nothing wrong with enjoying the pleasures of life, but there's everything wrong with having your life exist for your pleasure. In essence, when you overindulge, you devote yourself to your own desires.

When Paul describes the devotion that singleness enables, he calls it "undivided", meaning without distraction or diversion. It is meant to be exclusive. Your devotion to your hobbies or your career or your friends shouldn't compete with your devotion to God. You should enjoy the freedom you have as a single, but that freedom ultimately exists for you to mature in your relationship with God. You may not be held accountable by a spouse for the way you live your life, but you are being held accountable by the Lord.

Jesus says, "If anyone would come after me, let him deny himself and take up his cross and follow me. For whoever would save his life will lose it, but whoever loses his life for my sake will find it" (Matt. 16:24-25). In order to follow Jesus, we need to deny ourselves. This doesn't mean rejecting everything we love. It means that our relationship with Christ redefines our relationship to everything else. We are to enjoy singleness, yes, but not to the extent that it distracts us from our devotion to Christ. We might benefit from singleness, but singleness does not exist solely for our benefit.

THE LIE OF PREOCCUPATION

"Singleness exists so I can find love."

There are some singles I've talked with who sound like time travelers: all they talk about is their future spouse and future children they plan to have someday, thinking so much about the future they want that they seem blind to the present. Not everyone is as vocal, but these desires for a spouse and a family can still marinate in their minds to the point that it becomes all they think about.

Here, singleness is treated as a means to an end. We see our singleness less as a gift and more like a stepping stone, an in-between. It's like a train station: an uncomfortable place meant to be passed through to arrive at our true destination. The last thing we would want to consider is staying there for any longer than we have to. The sooner it ends, the better.

When we fall into this belief, we usually spend far more mental and emotional time in the world of love—real or aspirational—than we do the world of singleness. This often looks like reading romantic novels, spending significant amounts of time on dating apps, routinely looking at pictures on social media of someone you like, obsessing over other people's relationships, and compromising on boundaries while dating. Potential points of concern or red flags with dates are usually disregarded.

When we make our love life the point of singleness, we approach it from a place of fear rather than a place of freedom. We can see romantic prospects as saviors from singleness instead of human beings who have their own unique challenges and frustrations. Instead of caring about how God thinks of us, we care only how a potential partner thinks of us. Instead of working on our relationship with God, we work on improving our chances of finding romantic success. Our happiness becomes tied to our love life: when things are going well, we feel elated. When we encounter disappointment or heartbreak, we become full of despair and bitterness.

Worse, we become entitled. The more years you've been single, the more likely you believe you'll find your future spouse. Dating becomes spinning the wheel at the casino: the more you do it, the closer you think you'll win big. When you do find romantic happiness, it's because you've *earned* it rather than God *blessing* you with it.

When Paul unpacks the anxieties that come with marriage, he is saying "this for your own benefit, not to lay any restraint upon you" (1 Cor. 7:35). He isn't trying to hold you back from pursuing marriage. And yet, Paul believes his words are for your benefit. You can allow your desire for future marriage to overcome your appreciation for the present beauty in your singleness.

Paul continues, saying his words aren't meant to restrain you, "but to promote good order and to secure your undivided devotion to the Lord" (v. 35). By "good order", Paul is saying it puts our relationship with God into a proper and appropriate place. When we fall into the lie of preoccupation, we twist the good order by prioritizing romantic love above God's divine love. We devote ourselves to marriage instead of God.

The pursuit of marriage isn't fundamentally bad. Paul says as much a few verses earlier: "if you do marry, you have not sinned" (1 Cor. 7:28). However, when we make the pursuit the purpose, our trajectory becomes misaligned. Singleness wasn't made as a train station, it's a destination. A place where you can put down roots. Staying single longer than expected doesn't mean you're falling behind in life, it means the plan God has for your love life is different than yours.

THE LIE OF EVASION

"Singleness exists to protect me."

In addition to overindulgence or romantic obsession, we can also misuse the gift of singleness as a deflection from vulnerability. Singleness becomes characterized by avoidance of intimacy.

For some, this struggle is simply a fear of commitment. It's a "Peter Pan" mentality: a flight from having to "grow up".

We avoid the important stuff to deal with it later. We'll get around to it once we have more time, once we're older, once we're more religious, or once we're better established in our career. Unlike the lie of overindulgence, in which we avoid responsibility to preserve our own happiness, the lie of evasion is motivated by protecting ourselves from pain and vulnerability. We want to avoid feeling trapped. We want to keep our options open in case we want to escape. Often, this avoidance is maintained because we don't feel ready. We don't know what will happen if things don't go the way we think they should.

Many who believe this lie seek protection from deep emotional wounds. Singleness becomes a refuge from relational pain. I know of many singles who have survived intense breakups, abuse, embarrassing mistakes, heart-wrenching infidelity, and divorce. We escape into our singleness, afraid to come out. Vulnerability becomes limited, trust is carefully measured, and friendships are restricted.

There's a friend of mine I will call Barry. Twice, he has been through unwanted divorce. Because of his past pain, he finds himself in a dilemma. "I still long for a deep, intimate connection. But at the same time, because of my experience . . . I don't want to chance another divorce, another broken relationship."

However, Barry recognizes that this fear puts him directly at odds with the essence of human connection: "Relationship implies vulnerability. Vulnerability implies pain. I can avoid the pain, but in doing so I cut myself off from vulnerability which cuts me off from relationship."[1]

Barry's wise words point to the heart of this lie: in our attempts to avoid pain, we end up isolating ourselves from our own humanity. We think we're running toward singleness but in actuality we're running away from relationship. Instead of embracing singleness for what it is, we desire it for what it *isn't*. It isn't heartache, it isn't pain, it isn't emotional risk. Instead, it's a sanctuary.

You might have some openness to dating or marrying again, but there are strings attached. It would have to be on your terms. These one-sided "relationships" don't allow much room for surprises. Or mistakes. You do whatever you can to protect yourself from being surprised, and if things don't go according to plan, you immediately retreat into singleness, into yourself: a secret failsafe.

We need to remember Jesus deeply empathizes with our hurt because he, too, has been wounded by those he loves. The priests who should have seen him as the Son of God had him killed (Matt. 26:3-4), one of his loyal followers betrayed him (v. 48-50), and one of his closest friends openly denied knowing him multiple times (v. 74-75), all within the span of a day.

And still, having experienced deep pain, Jesus reassures us: "Peace I leave with you; my peace I give to you. Not as the world gives do I give to you. Let not your hearts be troubled, neither let them be afraid" (John 14:27). Though he was hurt relationally and though we are deeply flawed, Jesus still wants a relationship with us.

Paul desires us to "secure your undivided devotion to the Lord" (1 Cor. 7:35). It isn't about simply acquiring a devotion to God, but *securing* it, to have a stable and unwavering commitment to him. He never promises a painless life, but he does promise a purposeful one, without any regrets.

SINCERE AND PURE DEVOTION

There are so many ways in which we've twisted and abused singleness for our own purposes. Some of us may struggle with one lie more than the others. Or, if you're like me, you'll bounce from one to another. Fortunately for us, God is a good and loving God. He will never force you into something you don't want. The gift of singleness is much better than any alternative, but the choice of devoting yourself to Christ is yours alone to make.

It isn't about "having" or "not having" the gift of singleness, it's about seeking or not seeking intimacy with Jesus. When Paul refers to securing our devotion, he's connecting our fruitfulness in singleness to our relationship with God.

So, what exactly does godly devotion look like? If we're to focus on a relationship with God instead of a holy to-do list, it can seem difficult to know what the next step is. As it turns out, in his second letter to the Corinthians, Paul brings up devotion again. He is sharing a concern about false teachers, but the nature of his concern tells us more about how this might apply to our singleness.

> I am afraid that as the serpent deceived Eve by his cunning, your thoughts will be led astray from a sincere and pure devotion to Christ.
>
> (2 Cor. 11:3)

Paul makes a reference to Genesis, where Adam and Eve were forbidden to eat from the tree of the knowledge of good and evil. A serpent tricks Eve into eating the fruit of the tree. But how?

The serpent begins with a question: "Did God *really* say...?" (Gen. 3:1 NIV, emphasis mine). He is questioning Eve's trust, introducing doubt around God's very words. Whenever you doubt the truth, you become susceptible to trusting lies. A few verses later, the serpent builds upon the doubt he's planted. He tells Eve, "You will not surely die. For God knows that when you eat of [the tree] your eyes will be opened, and you will be like God, knowing good and evil" (Gen. 3:4-5).

The most effective deceptions are based on slivers of truth. The serpent was right in the sense that the man and the woman would know good and evil, but he left out the fact that they would introduce sin and agony into the world by doing so. What he said in the garden wasn't entirely false, but that didn't make it true.

Our singleness is no exception to this, either. When we see singleness as an excuse to gratify our desires, a means to find marriage, or a protection from commitment, we are taking the truth and twisting it to suit our needs. We *should* enjoy the freedom of singleness, but not to the point where we place our happiness above God. We *should* pursue marriage, but not to the point where our future spouse replaces God as our number one love. We *should* make room to find healing from emotional wounds, but not to the point where we isolate from everyone.

When Paul talks to the Corinthians, he expresses a desire for them to maintain a "sincere and pure devotion to Christ" (2 Cor. 11:3). God wants to use our singleness to deepen our devotion to him. While the gift tells us a lot about the gift-giver, what we do with the gift tells the giver a lot about us. So, let's use our gift to grow in our devotion to God.

Reflection Questions:

• What are you devoted to? What do you commit most of your time, your thoughts, and your money toward?

• Which of these three lies do you tend to struggle with the most? Which one are you struggling with right now, and how is it showing up in your daily life?

• Picture someone you know who has a "sincere and pure devotion to Christ" (2 Cor. 11:3). How have you seen that devotion play out in their life? How can you better embody your own devotion to Christ?

3

SINGLE . . . FOR LIFE?!

I never liked high school gym class. But the day it was run by the Marines is permanently etched in my memory.

It all started when my school district made the decision to give us an extra day off for Thanksgiving break. The trade-off? We would have class during Veteran's Day. To help justify this change, the rule was that each and every class would have to relate to American history in some way.

And for gym class, they brought in the Marines.

Having been told this ahead of time, I had a pit in my stomach the whole day. Other teenagers acted unfazed, insisting they had the stones to go toe-to-toe with any Marine. Not me. I knew my place. I'd seen the movies, and knew whatever they were going to throw at me, I wouldn't be ready. I wasn't out of shape, but I was far from a prime physical specimen. My plan was straightforward: blend in and be as compliant as possible.

Having changed into our uniforms, we all walked into the field house, where a contingent of Marines were waiting for us. They looked like a pack of wolves observing a herd of deer.

I began to execute my plan: standing far away from the rebellious-minded teens. I was talking with some of my buddies when one of the Marines approached our group. He pointed to several of us, including me.

"You, you, and you: follow me."

So much for blending in.

He made each of us stand in a line. Then, he called out to the rest of the class in a voice that could cleave continents. Using myself and the other "volunteers" as reference points, I watched as he single-handedly organized everyone into perfectly straight lines.

The rest of class ended up being fairly straightforward: each group would do a simple workout, like sit-ups or planks, for a minute, and then rotate to the next one. Each workout became progressively more challenging. My muscles began to ache and I thought I couldn't go on, but guess what? The next workout used an entirely different muscle group, one that had not yet been whipped into shape by the Marines. Every workout brought pain to a new part of my body. There were muscle groups I didn't know I had that were screaming in pain. It felt like I was waging war against my own body. By the time class ended, I had produced enough sweat to make another ocean.

We can experience struggles as singles in a similar way: an exhausting spiritual (and physical) ordeal that never seems to end, a battle where you face off against your own desires, and it feels like you're always losing. In the midst of this turmoil, you may ask yourself how much longer it will last. Does this pain have an expiration date, or will you have to endure it for the rest of your life?

AN UNCOMFORTABLE POSSIBILITY

"Celibacy" is an uncomfortable word, typically held in the same regard as "moist" or "soggy" or "taxes." It elicits strong negative reactions amongst those who hear it, mainly because it either sounds archaic or holier-than-thou. It might bring to mind images of monks, nuns, and Mother Theresa: spiritual role models that feel impossible to emulate. Most people associate a life without sex (and marriage) with joylessness and emptiness.

So, what's celibacy doing in a book for struggling romantics? As a struggling romantic myself, there's a temptation to gloss over or ignore the topic of celibacy altogether. But my discomfort toward celibacy doesn't nullify its importance. In fact, it *highlights* it. There are many singles who are afraid they'll never find someone to marry. Maybe it's a series of failed relationships. Maybe it's a deep ache for intimacy. One way or another, we respond to these difficulties by asking ourselves, "Will this ever end?" And then we wonder, "What if it *doesn't* end?" I would wager that, for a majority of us, we have only ever thought about celibacy in a context of fear and dread.

This fear is, in part, due to our culture, whose strong emphasis on sex makes it almost impossible to picture living without it. Another important factor is the limited teaching from churches on celibacy. Religious scholar Lauren F. Winner laments, "The sad thing is that there is very little space in today's evangelical churches for discerning a call to singleness."[1] My hope is this will help provide you that space.

People are staying single longer, and the United States Census confirms this. In 2023, the average age when couples got married was 30 years old for men and 28 years old for women.[2] Compare this to 2010, where it was 28 years old for men and 26 years old for women.[3] The average American citizen (and therefore the average American Christian) is staying single for longer periods of time.

I want to equip you for whatever path God has for you. For some of you, that might be lifelong singleness, and I want to honor that as a legitimate calling. Many of you will likely get married, but your fear of staying single is preventing you from delighting in the gift that it is. I don't want this for you. Whether for a season or for a lifetime, my goal is for you to delight in your singleness without any reservation or fear.

A NUANCED PICTURE

Celibacy can be an uncomfortable topic, but we still need to address it. Why? Because Jesus does so. There's a moment in the book of Matthew where he is speaking to the Pharisees about divorce. He firmly reminds them that marriage was designed to bring two lives into one. We'll explore this idea in a later chapter, but watch how the disciples respond to his words: "The disciples said to him, 'If such is the case of a man with his wife, it is better not to marry'" (Matt. 19:10).

The disciples' response is baffling. They don't cheer or pump their fists. Jesus' description of marriage doesn't stoke their enthusiasm, it gives them pause. They do what many of us might when we feel unable to comprehend an idea: they go to the extreme. If marriage was designed by God as a fixed commitment, with no intended room for divorce, then perhaps it's easier to abandon the idea of marriage altogether.

But [Jesus] said to them, "Not everyone can receive this saying, but only those to whom it is given. For there are eunuchs who have been so from birth, and there are eunuchs who have been made eunuchs by men, and there are eunuchs who have made themselves eunuchs for the sake of the kingdom of heaven. Let the one who is able to receive this receive it."

(Matt. 19:11-12)

Jesus doesn't say the disciples' hesitations are wrong, but he makes it clear that his remarks on marriage will be received by "only those to whom it is given." In other words, not everyone is meant for marriage, so it should not be pursued by everyone. So what about those who are unable to receive what Jesus is saying? What about those who lack strong sexual appetites or desires for marriage?

Jesus refers to different kinds of eunuchs, people who—put simply—couldn't physically reproduce. Without delving into historical detail, we can simply say that "eunuch" in this passage equates with a person who is single for life. Jesus acknowledges that eunuchs aren't a one-size-fits-all: they come from a variety of contexts. The reason one person remains single won't always be the same as another. Rebeca, a friend of mine, put it this way: "Different people experience being single differently."[4]

Let's dig deeper into the examples of eunuchs that Jesus gives, because they offer a more nuanced picture of celibacy than we may initially think. The first group are "eunuchs who have been so from birth." Some people have simply never had a strong desire to get married or to have sex. As far as marriage is concerned, they could take it or leave it.

If this is similar to how you feel, there is good news: Jesus is freeing you from feeling obligated to marry. This doesn't mean you are banned from marriage as an option, it means you have an opportunity that few others can easily take, without the distractions that married life (or unfulfilled sexual desire) brings. You have a unique capacity to dedicate yourself to a life of focused ministry.

The next category Jesus mentions are "eunuchs who have been made eunuchs by men." Typically, a eunuch was a man who had been castrated by a ruler. Translating this to a modern context, however, being made a eunuch by others could look a few different ways. Maybe you initially felt a desire toward marriage, but something happened that changed your priorities. Perhaps you experienced trauma or abuse that affected your desire for marriage or for sex.

If you fall into this category, allow me to add an important caveat: celibacy is not only a good gift for devoting yourself to ministry, but also a healthy space to heal from the trauma you've endured. Any work you do now to address your wounds will be a huge blessing to the churches or people you come into contact with. Besides, unless God has specifically said so, you may not be single forever. Be sure to discern what kind of healing work you need with the Lord, alongside wise counsel, as any residual hurt will carry over into your marriage if left untouched.

Finally, Jesus mentions a third group: "eunuchs who have made themselves eunuchs for the sake of the kingdom of heaven." These are individuals who voluntarily choose celibacy so they can dedicate their lives to God without distraction. Maybe you've been on a few dates or possess some desire for sexual intimacy but find yourself feeling a stronger desire to serve God to the best of your ability. The more you've stayed single, the more comfortable you are remaining that way.

This final group is what many of us struggling romantics typically confuse ourselves with. Sometimes you go on date after date, but the doors keep closing. Maybe you get excited about someone only to find out they're not a good fit for you. Does this mean you're being called to singleness, or are you just single because it's your own fault?

We need to look at the phrasing here: Jesus is describing eunuchs who "made themselves" that way for the sake of God's kingdom. We aren't forcibly enlisted into eunuch-hood, it's a voluntary choice. While we are all offered the gift of singleness, not all of us have a lifelong guarantee of singleness.

A LIFELONG SINGLE

Rebeca, whom I mentioned earlier, has a unique insight into celibacy. She is a consecrated virgin: a member of the Catholic Church who has sworn to live the rest of her life as a celibate. This isn't exclusive to Catholics: many Protestant men and women have made similar commitments.

"Some people assume celibates are monks or hermits," she muses, referring to the isolated and extreme lifestyles associated with those groups, but this couldn't be further from the truth. Rebeca lives in an ecumenical community, serving alongside believers from different denominational backgrounds who have made similar choices. She typically spends her days engaging in intercessory prayer and serving the poor. Given her community and her lifestyle, she has a fascinating perspective on practicing celibacy in the modern world.

We may assume people like Rebeca can only live the way they do because they don't have any sexual or romantic desires, but for Rebeca this isn't the case. She has desires for marriage, but she doesn't live under a rock: she is acutely aware that sex is a massive idol in our culture, affecting "the way we look at our own vocation to marriage or sexual identity." It can distort the way we discern a calling toward marriage or celibacy. Her main strategies for fighting temptation are prayer first, then community, then being careful with the media she consumes.

What impresses me about Rebeca is her ability to appreciate the beauty in both singleness and marriage. This has a lot to do with her story: she had a strong desire to be single, but felt that God wasn't blessing her pursuit. It wasn't until he opened her eyes to the allure of marriage that he finally blessed her original desire for singleness. Even then, she took several years of prayer and discernment before finally making her vow to lifelong celibacy.

Despite our misunderstandings, celibacy isn't as far-fetched or as old-fashioned as we may perceive it to be. You don't need to take a vow to live wholeheartedly single for the Lord. "Try living as if you were [a celibate] and see what happens," Rebeca says, "see if this way of life suits you."

There have been some people, she adds, who tried to live as lifelong celibates only to discover their desire for marriage was too strong. "If God hasn't given you grace from your desire [for marriage], then seek it out. It's a good and holy desire. You shouldn't make a lifelong commitment to celibacy if God doesn't give you grace."[5]

FEAR NOT

When I finally surrendered my life to Christ, I was terrified God would send me to live in Africa as a missionary. I know it sounds absurd, but I had always associated missions work with "super Christians". I wanted to follow God's calling for my life, and thought, hilariously, that doing so would inevitably result in moving to a third-world country. Because I thought missions was the pinnacle of faith, I feared that God would call me there.

Suffice it to say, I never moved to Africa. But years later, I met someone who had actually been called by God to do missions work there. Her story, however, was much different than mine. From a young age, she had a heart for Africa. She assumed everyone had the same desire until she talked to her friends in college and realized none of them felt the same passion about Africa that she felt. It was then that she began to wonder if God had given her this desire in order to lead her there.

God equips us for our callings. It doesn't mean it will be easy, but it means he will give us what we need to be sustained. Neither celibacy nor marriage can be done without God: both depend on our relationship with him. After he mentions the different eunuchs, Jesus says, "Let the one who is able to receive this receive it" (v. 11). If you don't consider yourself a eunuch in either of the ways Jesus describes, then you may not be called to celibacy. You need not fear it, just as I did not need to fear being called to missions work in Africa.

This does not negate the fact that, for now, whether for a few more days or years or decades, God has made you single. The gift of singleness isn't just for the "super Christians": it gives us freedom and flexibility to seek the Lord, to pursue a relationship with Jesus.

You aren't missing out on God's best by remaining single. Paul writes, "To the unmarried and the widows I say that it is good for them to remain single, as I am" (1 Cor. 7:8). Then, he continues, "But if they cannot exercise self-control, they should marry. For it is better to marry than to burn with passion" (1 Cor. 7:9). Desiring marriage isn't wrong: God made marriage! If you desire it, you haven't chosen an inferior path. Both celibacy and marriage bring glory to God. Neither is a waste of your life.

In wrestling with the prospect of lifelong singleness, we need to understand that everything ultimately comes down to God's timing, not ours. Often, we want to have a specific answer for the future of our love life, and often God doesn't give it to us. "Your word is a lamp to my feet and a light to my path" (Ps. 119:105). They didn't have powerful lights back in the days of the psalmist: instead, they only had candles and torches. The light at their feet only illuminated the next few steps, not the entire path. In the same way, we need to take it one day at a time, one step at a time.

You don't know what the future holds. Your years as a single could end at any point. You could experience an underwhelming first date, only for the second date to take a turn for the better. You could be convinced you'll be single for life, only to have someone cute appear whom you can't stop thinking about. You could end up getting married to someone who "wasn't your type" or whom you initially placed firmly in the friend zone. You never know.

I had a roommate who told me that dating was the furthest thing from his mind. I asked him if there was a woman he was interested in, and he said, "Not really. I want to pursue a career in ministry and feel like dating would hold me back in that regard." The following month, he started dating a woman who eventually became his wife. Clearly, God had different plans for his ministry career. When God is the one writing your love story, all you can do is expect the unexpected.

God isn't looking for a "super Christian": he's looking for a personal relationship with you. At the end of the day, it's our faith in Jesus and our desire for God that sustains us. Biblical singleness is not necessarily about being satisfied with singleness, it's about being necessarily satisfied with God.

Reflection Questions:

• Do you wrestle with the possibility of staying single for the rest of your life? What would be terrifying or exciting about this possibility?

• Read Matthew 19:11-12. What confuses or comforts you about Jesus' description of the eunuchs?

• Read Psalm 63. How has God satisfied you in your life? In your singleness? How can you seek a greater satisfaction in him?

4

MARRIAGE MANIA

I have a strange history with video games.

Back in high school, I bought my first ever video game console and quickly got sucked in. Most nights, I would play until around two in the morning. At some point, I realized that video games were taking over my life, so I ended up selling them all online. For a time, there was peace. My life returned to normal. Nature began to heal.

Then, several years later, I got my first job. Money was easier to come by. I went out and bought my second video game console: a PlayStation 3.

This time, it will be different, I told myself. *I'm older now, I can resist becoming addicted again.* But almost immediately, I went back to staying up all night, the video games I controlled once again controlling me. Something needed to change, and fast.

I decided to go to my father for help.

"Dad," I asked, "Do you have a sledgehammer I could borrow?"

"What for?"

"I want to destroy my PlayStation with it."

Without batting an eye, he said, "I don't have a sledgehammer, but you can use my axe."

"That works."

And so, my brother and I took the PlayStation outside and whaled on it with Dad's axe, freeing me from my proverbial bonds. To this very day, one of the joysticks from the PlayStation controller sits on my desk: the remainder of a modern-day cautionary tale.

Obsessively playing video games isn't seen as a life-changing addiction so much as a nuisance. On the surface, this makes sense: unlike drugs, video games don't induce debilitating withdrawal symptoms, cause street gangs to kill each other over them, and lead to people getting arrested for possessing them. But the spiritual effects are real, and because we see such obsessions as essentially harmless, we don't often confront them. Your parents might get frustrated if your grades drop, your non-gaming friends might struggle to get a hold of you at times, but the accountability rarely goes beyond that.

Marriage can become a similarly addicting obsession that is often downplayed or even praised. It's a fixation I call "marriage mania." Rather than a fixation on the *experience* of being married, marriage mania is a fixation on the *idea* of being married. Marshall Segal describes how this affected him in his single years:

> I didn't experiment with marijuana or go through a
> drinking phase. My drug of choice was more socially
> acceptable, even encouraged. I was recklessly trying to feed
> my heart's hunger for God by running after romance and
> intimacy.[1]

Marriage mania happens when we mistake marriage as our salvation—our escape—from singleness. When we feel lonely or despair in singleness, we think about the romance, companionship, and intimacy we'll have in marriage as a way to soothe the pain. In our secular culture, there are other ways to experience these things outside of marriage, namely through cohabitation and casual sexual encounters. But within Christendom, where such things are limited to marriage, we can fixate on our wedding day as being the source of sexual and relational liberation, the ultimate solution to the "problem" of singleness.

MARRIAGE AS ALL OR NOTHING

As struggling romantics, it's important to start with the end in mind. If we desire to be married someday, it's essential for us to understand what we'll be committing ourselves to. Besides, we cannot fully appreciate singleness without also appreciating marriage. No matter what is in our future, when we understand the created intent behind one, we can better understand the design of the other.

As someone who has been to many weddings and had in-depth discussions with several married couples, I can tell you that marriage is beautiful. There's a good reason we desire it as struggling romantics. Everything, from intimacy to love to companionship, is intensified and deepened. This is also what makes marriage challenging at times: it isn't just love through feelings toward one another, but love within a lifelong covenant. Through the honoring of this commitment and mutual dedication to each other, marriage can be a catalyst for incredible growth, maturity, and transformation in the lives of both spouses.

Marriage is good, and desiring it doesn't make you a marriage maniac. So, what does? Fundamentally, marriage mania is an "all or nothing" mentality in which marriage has it all and singleness has nothing. For example, within marriage you experience a level of growth and maturity that you can't as a single. Marriage mania, however, convinces us that marriage is the *only* avenue by which we can grow and mature. Since singleness cannot offer the same depth and intimacy as marriage, marriage mania tells us we will never experience *any* meaningful depth or intimacy as singles. If marriage has it, singleness doesn't. If both have it, marriage offers the version you want more.

So how exactly does this disrupt our lives? In order to answer this, I want to revisit my struggle with video games. There was one game in particular I obsessed over: a fantasy game where you could be any character you wanted to be and explore any part of the world at your leisure. I was totally immersed and would play it as soon as I returned home from school. I would sneak downstairs to play it late at night, long after the rest of my family had gone to bed. No matter where I went, from school to home to hanging out with friends, all I thought about was the next time I could play the game. It wasn't some fun recreational hobby: it had become the center of my life.

Because of my obsession with that game, I despised everything that threatened my time with it. If my grades were low and my parents took away my video game privileges, I treated them as my mortal enemies. If there was a family dinner or church event in the evening, I was less excited to go because it interfered with my game time. In other words, everything that prohibited or delayed the object of my obsession was seen as an obstacle.

We can obsess over marriage to an even greater degree. When marriage is all that we can see, our singleness feels prohibitive, like it's an obstacle between us and our happiness. When we believe that marriage is the solution, then singleness looks a lot more like the problem. Marriage mania ends up putting unhealthy pressure on finding romantic fulfillment. When we think marriage will resolve all our problems, then the thought of being married becomes all we think about. The gift of singleness becomes the hurdle of singleness.

MARRIAGE AS AN ANTIDOTE

American culture promotes a similar obsession, replacing marriage with relationships instead. For all its pro-singleness rhetoric, there remains a "pro-romance" undercurrent that hasn't gone away. It's okay for you to be single—so long as you have someone you can be single with. We remain fixated on sexual satisfaction and see romantic relationships as a path toward deeper friendship, instead of the other way around.

This thinking has trickled into the western church as well. Of course, instead of "pro-romance", the message has been reshaped into "pro-marriage." This isn't wrong, strictly speaking: again, marriage is a good gift from God. But most churches make no distinction between a natural desire for marriage and an idolization of it: any craving for marriage in any amount is implicitly assumed to be healthy.

Furthermore, there are small, subconscious messages within the majority of church culture that can make singles feel isolated instead of accepted. When marriage is presented as preferable, the implication is that being unmarried is undesirable. John Chapman, an unmarried Australian preacher, unpacks specific ways in which these messages can be unintentionally communicated:

> When describing the nature of your church please don't exclude me by saying, "This is a family-oriented church." You could as easily say, "We aim to cater to all ages of people here at this church." I'll feel as if I belong then. If you invite single people to dinner, don't feel you have to "match" them with someone else at dinner. It is possible to have odd numbers.[2]

The mania's "all or nothing" mentality makes marriage the de facto "solution" to singleness's aches and agonies. Singleness is seen as a poison you have to grin and bear, while marriage provides the antidote. In conversation, marriage is often treated as a cure-all for singleness-related ailments:

• Do you struggle with a deep yearning for marriage? Find a spouse already so you can stop being distracted by your hormones.

• Are you promiscuous and sleep around? Get married so you can have someone to keep you in check.

• Are you lonely and sad? Get married so you can have someone in your life who makes you feel happy.

• Do you wrestle with same-sex attraction? Marry someone of the opposite sex so your desires can be properly expressed.

• Are you irresponsible? Get married so your lifestyle improves and you can become a proper man or woman.

Note the toxic simplicity of these prescriptions. Spiritual disciplines such as prayer, scripture, and fasting are not considered serious remedies, nor is the option of remaining single: marriage is depicted as the only legitimate fix. The savior from burdens and struggles becomes the spouse, not the Christ.

When we desire marriage, we desire something good and God-given. After all, "he who finds a wife finds a good thing and obtains favor from the Lord" (Prov. 18:22). But when our desire is all that we can see and marriage becomes "all or nothing" to us, our search becomes fueled by either self-preservation or self-gratification. And neither of those are healthy reasons to get married.

MARRIAGE DEMOTED

When we wrongly perceive marriage as a "fix" for singleness, we ironically demote it. Instead of a sacred commitment, marriage becomes a rite of passage. It's no longer a blessing, it's a milestone: an expectation instead of a gift from God. When we normalize marriage to this degree, it becomes trivialized.

The results are disastrous, not only for marriages (as discussed above), but also for singles for two main reasons. First, singles are assumed to be less mature. Because marriage is the "next step" for adults to take, people who remain unmarried are seen as less responsible and "behind" in life. If you're still single after most of your peers are married, something must be wrong with you. Married couples, by comparison, are seen as more responsible and put-together. Consequently, singles are treated as second-class citizens.

One example of this was a worship pastor I knew. As part of his job, he would often hold auditions at his church for students. While he was single, he would often receive emails from parents of some of the female students who wanted to ensure their daughters weren't alone with him. Once he got married, however, those emails stopped. He hadn't changed the way he held auditions—his wife wasn't even with him most of the time—but the concerns had evaporated. Parents trusted him more simply because of his marital status. Once he was married, an assumption was made that he was more mature and less of a risk.

Secondly, framing marriage as the only solution for singleness puts immense pressure on finding a spouse quickly. Taking your time to ensure you find a quality spouse feels less appealing: if you wait, you may miss out on your future wife or husband. Choosing to remain single, be it for a season or a lifetime, is seen as good-intentioned but ultimately shortsighted. The goal is to find a spouse before time runs out, before the option is gone forever. It doesn't matter how ready you feel you need to be; it's less about "getting it right" beforehand and more about taking the plunge.

As a result, dating becomes a rat race fueled by desperation to find anyone who is remotely suitable. Time feels like it's running out the older you get and the more failed relationships you experience. Ultimately, when marriage is an expectation, it ceases to be the beautiful gift it is, one God gives according to his timeline, not ours.

THE FEAR BEHIND THE MANIA

As you could probably tell from my Introduction, I was the quintessential marriage maniac. For years, marriage was on my mind almost all the time (which isn't much of an exaggeration). I would go to certain social events based on how likely I was to find my future wife there. Almost every woman who crossed my path made me immediately wonder "could she be my future spouse?"

Then, in high school, I made a decision that seemed to contradict all of that. On my own, I made a promise to the small group I was in that I wouldn't date at all while I was in high school. As my thinking went, college students were more mature than high school students, so the odds I would find my wife in college were greater than they were in high school.

"Well, gee," you're probably thinking, "look who's up high in his ivory tower. I should throw this book away since I can't contend with Mr. Perfect over here. My high school years looked like sin compared to yours!"

It may have seemed that way on the surface. From freshmen year to senior year, I didn't go on any dates, didn't have any girlfriends, and didn't so much as smooch anyone. But underneath, things couldn't have been further from the truth: my marriage mania continued unrestrained. I still thought about marriage nonstop. I still considered every woman I saw. I never went on a physical date, but I emotionally dated any woman I could, subconsciously offering my heart to those who gave it attention. My thought process wasn't "I'm not allowed to date so I won't think about it." It was "I'm not allowed to date unless someone I can't ignore comes along."

I struggled to fully give my singleness over to God because I was afraid. I was scared I would miss my future wife if I looked away for a single second (pun intended). I was scared that if I withdrew any amount of energy from my marriage search, then I would risk never getting married at all.

There is emotional fuel behind every obsession, and marriage mania is primarily powered by fear. We can sacrifice time in scripture for more swipes on a dating app, or avoid befriending those who aren't obvious romantic prospects. When we make decisions such as these, we are being controlled by our desire. More specifically, we're being controlled by fear that if we don't do something, our desire will remain unfulfilled. We need to find the right person as soon as possible. The onus is on *our* provision instead of God's.

We can also see failure as wasteful, whether it's an ugly breakup, an engagement that ended abruptly, an unwanted divorce, or a history of disappointing dates. We can feel as though we're missing out on what we're supposed to do, that all that time was for nothing.

But nothing is wasted with God. The breakups, the divorces, the mistakes . . . none of it is for nothing. Nothing given to him ever goes unused, whether it's our time, our resources, our desires, or our pain. When we have a relationship with Christ, we can trust him with our desires, because "in all things God works for the good of those who love him, who have been called according to his purpose" (Rom. 8:28 NIV). Consequently, our singleness is not for nothing, either. My friend Rebeca frames it this way: "If you're seeking the Lord and being vulnerable with him and diving deep into your faith, you're not going to miss what he has for you."[3] Isn't that comforting? So long as you seek God, you can't lose.

I saw this in my half-hearted decision to not date in high school. In spite of my hypocrisy and the monument to marriage my heart had built, God was still able to redeem my pursuit of marriage into a pursuit of him. As my story hopefully shows, when you offer a sacrifice to God, even if you don't do it "right", God still shows up. He still moves.

God loves you, but he isn't you. Because he isn't you, he will love you in ways you will not expect or always appreciate at the time. He reminds us, "As the heavens are higher than the earth, so are my ways higher than your ways and my thoughts than your thoughts" (Isa. 55:9). God will love you in ways that may not feel like love in the moment, including keeping you single longer than you want and exposing the idols you have in your life.

Marriage is a good thing to seek with God, but it's a bad thing to replace him with. As Nancy Wilson points out, "Marriage is a means, not an end. It is one of the means God uses to glorify His name among us, but it is not His only means."[4] Marriage is not the fulfillment of singleness, nor is it the point: God is. We can live a full life with or without marriage because it isn't marriage that gives us meaning—it's God. Marshall Segal describes it this way:

> God does not guarantee any human experience for his
> children—not physical health, not marriage, not success at
> work, not children. And that's because he is utterly,

relentlessly committed to giving his precious sons and daughters what's best for them, when it's best for them, and only if it's best for them.[5]

You aren't missing anything: you're right where you need to be. Being single doesn't make you less mature or more flawed: you're just as beloved as everyone else. Instead of obsessing about finding a spouse, we ought to see singleness for the blessing that it is, and God for the good father that he is. Rest in the fact that he has your best in mind. Don't fixate on the gift you want to the point where you miss the gift you already have.

Reflection Questions:

• Have you ever become obsessed with something to the point where it negatively impacted your life? How did you recognize it was a problem?

• Would you label yourself a "marriage maniac"? Why or why not?

• Have you felt pressure to find a spouse? Have you ever felt you were "lesser" because you were single? How has that pressure or judgment affected your perception of your singleness?

5

FALLING FOR A CARICATURE

I thought we had chemistry together.

Well, in one sense, we did: Samantha and I were in the same chemistry class. But instead of oxygen and hydrogen, I wondered how the elements of her personality and mine would react when combined. After overthinking about it, I finally decided to ask Samantha out on a date. As soon as class ended and she left the room, I followed her outside and asked if we could talk.

My heart was racing and my legs were trembling. I was like a tree in the throes of a hurricane. Finally, I forced the words out of my mouth. "Would you like to get dinner sometime?"

"Sure," she said. My jaw hit the floor. I couldn't believe it!

We made plans to sit together in the dining hall, and I arrived early. I grabbed my food and found a seat, my eyes searching the room for Samantha.

Then, I saw her.

Samantha was stunning. Her hair was done, her eyes were covered in eyeliner, and she wore what looked like a brand new leather jacket. It seemed like overkill for the dining hall, but I was flattered she put in that much effort for me.

The heavenly being brought her food over and sat with me. We began to engage in small talk as we ate our generic cafeteria food. Then, just as I felt our conversation picking up momentum, Samantha began picking up her things to leave.

"I have a photo shoot scheduled for tonight," she said, as if she could see the questions forming in my mind. *That's why she looked so nice,* I thought. As she walked away, I was speechless for the second time that night. When we planned to have dinner together, neither Samantha nor myself ever used the word "date." Because I had assumed we were on the same page and because of her stunning appearance, I never questioned if my hopes were real. Because I only saw what I wanted to see, I ended up falling for a caricature I created in my mind.

Even if you don't know exactly what a caricature is, there's a good chance you've seen one before: an artistic style exaggerating the distinctive features of its subjects. You can find caricatures as favored styles amongst boardwalk artists and political cartoonists. Some credit Annibale Carracci from the 16th century as having invented the form. He is quoted describing his work as such:

> The [classical artist] may strive to visualise the perfect form and to realise it in his work, the [caricaturist] to grasp the perfect deformity, and thus reveal the very essence of a personality. A good caricature, like every work of art, is more true to life than reality itself.[1]

A caricature isn't an outright lie, it's a distortion. Certain qualities are emphasized while others are minimized. And yet, the power—and danger—of a caricature lies in how it can feel realer than real. It can make its subject appear irresistible or detestable, depending on whether the artist emphasizes the beauty or the flaws.

While he likely didn't intend for his remarks to be interpreted theologically, Carracci's commentary just as easily describes how we distort our perceptions of marriage. All too often, we can romanticize the desirable attributes of marriage and minimize the undesirable ones. In other words, the thing we fall in love with isn't actually marriage, but a fabrication that feels "more true to life than reality itself."

If marriage mania shapes our *pursuit* of marriage, then caricaturizing marriage shapes our *perception* of marriage—something that *feels* like marriage, but is actually a false representation. This can lead to nasty surprises down the road. We can expect an ideal friend who always attentively listens to our heart. We can expect a sexual companion that fulfills our every desire. Then, when those expectations fall short, we think, "Wait, what? I didn't sign up for this!" By removing the distortion, we can fully appreciate and better anticipate marriage within its proper context.

EXAMINING OUR DISTORTIONS

We tend to caricaturize marriage in two prominent ways. The first and most common way is when we exaggerate the benefits of marriage. We look at married couples and see the hand-holding, the cute photos, and the smiles on their wedding day. We hear stories where someone's spouse does something thoughtful or takes them on a fun night out. We imagine the committed love couples feel for each other and the sex they get to enjoy as a result of that intimacy. When we compare this to our singleness, we find our lives wanting. We end up feeling unloved, undesired, and unfulfilled.

When we accentuate the desirable aspects of marriage, it becomes a kind of nirvana in our mind's eye, a "heaven" we go to when we leave singleness behind. Marriage's companionship is a cure for loneliness, its intimacy a limitless source of sexual fulfillment, and its covenant a guaranteed safeguard against heartbreak. Once married, we'll never have to fear breakups or celibacy or isolation ever again. We'll spend the rest of our days with a person who understands us and sees our innermost needs before we ever have to ask. Of course marriage isn't perfect, but it seems pretty darn close.

But the knife of caricature cuts both ways. The second caricature of marriage is when we exaggerate its downsides instead, allowing cynicism to dominate our perception. We look at older married couples whose "love" for each other seems more like years of pent-up bitterness. Stories of abuse, rampant divorce, emotional distancing, and infidelity can make us wonder if marriage is nothing more than inevitable disappointment and relational failure. Instead of idealizing marriage, we vilify it. So, we avoid the commitment of marriage, even if we yearn to indulge in its "perks".

Of course, neither one of these views are accurate. Marriage is neither perfection nor a prison, and if we're not careful, we can slip from one caricature into another. In fact, when we caricaturize marriage, we often caricaturize our singleness in the opposite way. If marriage is heaven, singleness is hell; if marriage is emotionally risky, singleness is emotionally safe; if marriage is sexually fulfilling, singleness is sexually frustrating . . . and vice versa. We can flip-flop between the two like a seesaw.

Singles aren't the only ones who struggle with such caricatures: married couples do the same with singleness. In their lowest moments, married couples can feel a yearning for their single years. One couple admitted this to me, much to my surprise. I decided to dig deeper, so I asked, "In those moments, what about singleness made it so appealing?"

"You have so much freedom!" one of them replied. "You can do whatever you want to do, whenever you want to do it. There are times when I yearn for that flexibility and independence." This was not at all what I had expected: it was a cherry-picked perspective of singleness that, while not entirely wrong, was far from the complete experience. Sure, I can stay up as late as I want, but I'll always return to a lonely apartment. I can date anyone I please, but that person could leave at any moment because they aren't obligated to stay by my side. This married couple was wrestling with a false understanding of singleness that felt real to them.

It can be easier to see the fallacy of caricature when we experience it from the other side. If you romanticize marriage, what's going to stop you from romanticizing singleness once you get married? It's like the phrase "the grass is always greener on the other side."

But, as a friend pointed out to me, "It's always greener where you choose to water it." As singles, many of us seek marriage's blessings without fully understanding their purpose, which is dangerous to our future marriages and detrimental to our present singleness. At the end of the day, we are chasing after something that feels like marriage, but *isn't* marriage. As we've seen, singles and marrieds, alike, fall for caricatures; if we want to know what it is we're truly pursuing or fleeing, we need an accurate grounding of what marriage is.

MARRIAGE AS A FANTASYLAND

Marriage has many blessings that singleness doesn't, but it's also a lot harder. It takes a *lot* of effort to make a marriage work. You will be sharing your entire life with a flawed human being made in the image of God. That means some days you'll see them reflect the image of God, while other days you'll see the brokenness. As a result, married couples experience higher highs and lower lows. One person described marriage to me as "a maximum happiness of ten, and a maximum pain of negative ten." Your spouse will encourage you like no one else, but they will also hurt you like no one else. There will be times where you can't wait to see them, and times where both your patience and your capacity to forgive will be pushed to their utmost limits.

Both marriage and singleness are beautiful in their own ways, but because of the broken state of creation each has its own temptations and challenges. Neither will fully relieve you from stress or loneliness or temptation.

The danger of emphasizing the highs of marriage is that we can expect marriage to be enjoyable all the time, and then we will see the lows as evidence that we're in the wrong marriage. We can begin to believe marriage exists primarily to make us happy and satisfy our desires. If we try our best as a husband or a wife, then we assume our spouse will always and equally reciprocate. If we have needs, of course our spouse will always ensure they get met. Marriage becomes a magical realm in which our fantasies—physical, sexual, mental, emotional, and spiritual—are fulfilled perfectly and promptly.

Yet, the hard truth is that marriage does not exist to fulfill your fantasies. Take the realm of physical intimacy. There are countless stories of spouses having to work through their "sex-pectations": sometimes one of them is aroused while the other isn't in the mood. There will be differences in desires for the frequency of sex and the type of sex that each person is comfortable with. One spouse may have sexual trauma that will affect how sex is approached, or fantasies that the other person isn't comfortable fulfilling. This doesn't mean that marital sex is joyless: that would fall into the opposite caricature. It just means self-control doesn't go out the window once you get married. True happiness in marriage isn't *your* happiness, it's the *both* of you working to make each other happy.

Marriage won't cure your loneliness, either. Although "the two shall become one flesh" (Matt. 19:5), your individual differences will remain. There will still be struggles each of you experience differently. One of you may struggle with a mental illness that the other doesn't have or anxiety about things that don't bother the other person. Your spouse may have difficulties empathizing with you to the extent you're looking for. Sometimes, they may leave for a business trip or a weekend with friends, physically leaving you on your own. If you can't navigate loneliness as a single, you will have a difficult time facing it in your future marriage.

THE SACRIFICIAL CENTER

Are you even allowed to be happy in marriage? Of course you are. Marriage has joy and delight I can never experience as a single. Happiness is a part of marriage, but it isn't the *point* of marriage. How so? Because marriage is centered on sacrificial love. There is a selflessness woven into the design of marriage. We see this at wedding ceremonies, where the bride and groom traditionally stand in front of the wedding altar—a structure used to offer sacrifices.

There will be times where you will have to give up your free time, your money, your desires, and your sleep in order to love your spouse well. One example of this was a married couple where the wife had a chronic health condition. If she didn't take her medication, she experienced incredible pain. One time, she lost access to her medicine. During those weeks, she would scream in pain throughout the night. She couldn't even get out of bed and walk. Her husband stayed awake with her: praying, getting her water, and researching new medicines she could take.

This side of marriage isn't beautiful in a sexy or glamorous sense, but it's profoundly beautiful in a sacrificial sense. These moments are why understanding the sacrificial essence of marriage is so important. When trials come, we will be more willing to serve because we will be expecting to serve instead of being served.

If it sounds like I'm saying marriage is terrible, I'm not. Marriage is amazing and wonderful. I have friends who have routinely told me how happy they are being married. Christ-centered marriage is one of the most beautiful things on this side of heaven, but we need to know the immense responsibility that comes with that beauty. If all we see is the happiness of marriage, we will not understand the work and sacrifice required to maintain that happiness. We need to see marriage not only as sex, dates, and blissful nights cuddling on the couch, but also as a lifelong labor of love. Golf courses have the best-looking lawns, but they take countless hours of maintenance to maintain. In a similar way, the happiest marriages require continual work.

Think of when Jesus washed his disciples' feet (John 13:1-17). Culturally, he was humiliating himself: only the lowly servants would wash people's feet. It wasn't glamorous, especially when people wore sandals and their feet would accumulate dirt and grime from the roads. Furthermore, the people whose feet he washed were about to hurt him: Judas was about to betray him, and Peter was about to deny knowing him. Jesus knew these things, and yet, he washed their feet anyway. While Jesus' actions weren't glamorous, they were beautiful in a profoundly deep and sacrificial way.

Marriage isn't always easy, but when it is centered on God it is powerful and moving in a way that no movie or wedding photo can fully capture.

A FORESHADOWING OF ETERNITY

My parents and I were on our way to the car. We had spent a fun afternoon with some family friends, and I enjoyed goofing off with their kids. Before I made it to the car, however, their mother stopped me.

"I want to give you something," she said. She pulled out a twenty-dollar bill and offered it to me. "Thank you so much for spending time with my kids, it really meant a lot to me."

My mind was racing. I didn't want to accept her money, especially when I did nothing other than goof around. I was about to do the noble thing and turn down her gift, but my dad, who had seen the entire thing, stopped me before I could leave. "Go ahead and take the money," he said. Hesitantly, and only because my dad said so, I accepted the money and thanked her.

In the car, Dad clarified why he had intervened. "She was giving you the money as her way of showing her appreciation," he said, "And you were trying to shut down her only means of expressing gratitude to you." All I saw in the moment was the cost, but my dad opened my eyes to the heart behind it.

For some of us struggling romantics, we may be on the fence of accepting marriage because of its cost. After all, marriages only last, as the vows remind us, "until death do us part." One of you will become single again. Is marriage even worth it to begin with?

When we think in this way, we are looking at the twenty-dollar bill instead of the heart behind it, instead of the God behind it. Marriage isn't all heartbreak and difficulty, it's sacred. It points to a greater purpose. The earthly side of marriage—the finite side—will go away, but there is an eternal side that will never leave. Marriage is a symbol—a foretaste—of the eventual marriage of Christ and the Church.

> In the same way husbands should love their wives as their own bodies. He who loves his wife loves himself. For no one ever hated his own flesh, but nourishes and cherishes it, just as Christ does the church, because we are members of his body. "Therefore a man shall leave his father and

mother and hold fast to his wife, and the two shall become one flesh." This mystery is profound, and I am saying that it refers to Christ and the church.

(Eph. 5:28-32)

Just as we are made in the image of God and reflect his character, the joining together of husband and wife reflect the divine unity Christ has with the Church, and the joining of them that will soon come. This means that how we engage with our future spouse should reflect how Christ engages with his church. How does Christ love his bride? He offered his own life for our benefit, sacrificing himself without compromise, without hesitation, and without changing his mind. Our marriages are designed to reinforce this: a tangible foretaste of the eternal reality to come.

Scripture is clear that marriages on earth do not carry over into eternity. As Jesus points out, "in the resurrection they neither marry nor are given in marriage, but are like angels in heaven" (Matt. 22:30). Since angels serve the Lord and do not marry, our lives in heaven will become like theirs, at least in that regard. Earthly marriage won't be necessary—we will no longer need the symbol once we have what it represents.

For me, someone who has a deep desire to someday be married, this concept was difficult to understand, let alone embrace. God gave me a desire for marriage, yet, in eternity it will remain unfulfilled? However, in his book *Heaven*, Randy Alcorn shows that this couldn't be further from the truth. Our future marriage to Christ isn't something to dread, it's something incredibly exciting.

The one-flesh marital union we know on Earth is a signpost pointing to our relationship with Christ as our bridegroom.

> Once we reach the destination, the signpost becomes unnecessary. That one marriage—our marriage to Christ—will be so completely satisfying that even the most wonderful earthly marriage couldn't be as fulfilling . . .
> Here on Earth we long for a perfect marriage. That's exactly what we'll have—a perfect marriage with Christ.[2]

Someday, your dreams of a perfect marriage will come true, just not here on earth. In Christ and Christ alone lies the fulfillment and love you're looking for. He is the Original Romantic: marriage was his idea and his invention. No man or woman can fill what Christ can. If you struggle with cynicism toward marriage, this is good news for you, as well. Christ is the lover who knows and empathizes with you perfectly. An eternity with him isn't confining, it's freeing.

CORRECTING THE CARICATURE

Caricatures are dangerous because they are lies based in truth: it's why they feel "realer than real." The reality is that marriage is a symbol of Christ's sacrificial love and his eventual union with the church, and we can either confuse the symbol for Christ, or fixate on the human brokenness and neglect the sacred beauty the symbol points to.

If you struggle with a caricature of cynicism, know this: marriage is God's idea. It's an institution he has blessed, and there is a beauty within it that we, as singles, cannot completely understand because we haven't experienced it. If you struggle with a caricature of idealizing marriage, know this: marriage is a finite representation of an infinite beauty, an imperfect foretaste of a perfect love. If we expect marriage to satisfy all our desires, we're setting up our future marriage to fail. If we make our future spouse the source of our self-worth, we will be shouldering them with more expectations than they will ever be able to meet. But if Christ is at its center, he will work in spite of your human brokenness, but only if you allow him to.

By understanding the purpose of marriage, we should be more measured in our pursuit of it. Think about the times you've bought something expensive like a computer, a car, or a house. Before you buy it, it's normal to spend a lot of time thinking over your decision. Why? Because they are significant financial commitments. If this is true about cars or houses or computers, how much more time should you spend considering marriage? Not only is marriage a financial commitment, it's an emotional, physical, mental, and spiritual commitment, as well. Deciding to marry someone is a process that should be done thoughtfully and wisely.

Many people have said, "Don't worry, you'll find someone someday!" In other words, they try reassuring me that marriage is a certainty. In an earthly sense, they're wrong: no one's romantic future is guaranteed.

But in an eternal sense, they're spot on.

Reflection Questions:
- How have you exaggerated marriage into a caricature? Do you tend to highlight its benefits or its downsides?
- How have you exaggerated singleness into a caricature? What aspects might you be distorting?
- Do you know of any married couples whose relationship is centered on Christ? What does sacrificial love look like in their relationship?

6

WRITING YOUR LOVE STORY

Whenever someone meets a married couple, you can always count on one question being asked . . .

"How did you two meet?"

The answer they give describes the beginnings of their relationship. Maybe it was a meet-cute at a train station, a budding friendship in a small group, or a college rivalry that became romantic. Maybe it was "love at first sight" or maybe they knew each other years before dating.

How we start our relationships can have a powerful effect on how they grow. In our faith, the most powerful and personal tool you possess is your testimony, the story of how you began your relationship with Jesus. You started out in a place far from God, had an encounter with him, and now your life has never been the same. Testimonies point to the foundation of where your faith took root. Like the stories of how married couples met, testimonies are varied and yet all point to a common ending: a relationship with Christ.

While they might seem unrelated, both of these tales are examples of "founding stories". They may differ in how they're told, but they all answer the question of how something began. As humans, we are captivated by stories like these. We recognize there's something significant about the place something grows from, and what caused that growth in the first place. When we ask someone "how did you get to know your spouse?" or "what brought you together?", we are asking them for their founding story.

As struggling romantics, we have a unique opportunity to consider what kind of founding story we want for our marriage. This isn't a matter of deciding if you want to find your future spouse at a Walmart or at a church service. This is a question of what you want your story to say about you and your marriage, and what it will be built upon.

Imagine, if you will, a future in which you are married and are asked the question "How did you two meet?" What do you hope your answer will say about you and your spouse? About God's role in your life? About the values your marriage is founded on?

BUILDING ON ROCK OR SAND

In the first few chapters, we established that the purpose of singleness is to cultivate a pure devotion to Jesus. It should come as no surprise, then, that devotion to Christ is the foundation on which all godly marriages should be built. So, how can we apply that devotion to our founding story?

Founding stories explain the "why" behind relationships, but we usually think about these stories *after* they happen, not *before*. As we make new friends, pursue job opportunities, and seek a spouse, we are in the middle of making new founding stories, great and small. In order to learn what makes a founding story powerful, and how it affects our relationships, we must look at the book of Matthew, where

Jesus gives a parable about two men who build on different foundations.

> Everyone then who hears these words of mine and does them will be like a wise man who built his house on the rock. And the rain fell, and the floods came, and the winds blew and beat on that house, but it did not fall, because it had been founded on the rock.

> (Matt. 7:24-25)

If you're like me, you can gloss over this part and say, "We get it: the foundation of rock is good. Let's move on." But notice what the foundation of rock represents: it's whoever hears Jesus' words *and does them.* Building a healthy foundation requires that we respond to the words of God by allowing them to affect and dictate the way we live.

Listening to a convicting sermon from a pastor or wise advice from a friend isn't enough: we also need to follow through and make changes accordingly. When we do so, will our lives be comfortable and easy? No! There will be storms, rain, and violent winds, but so long as our foundation is in Christ—and living in a way that reflects him—what we build, based on him, will never crumble.

> And everyone who hears these words of mine and does not do them will be like a foolish man who built his house on the sand. And the rain fell, and the floods came, and the winds blew and beat against that house, and it fell, and great was the fall of it.

> (Matt. 7:26-27)

You could have the godliest friends, attend the best church, and know the Bible forward and backward, but if you don't apply the words and wisdom of God, none of that will matter.

When Jesus describes the house built on rock and the house built on sand, he doesn't focus on the size or quality of the house's construction. He doesn't say whether the men constructed a shack or a mansion or if they made their houses out of marble or wood. Why? Because no matter how big your house is or how great its materials are, it all falls apart if it's built on a faulty foundation. One writer put it bluntly: "Breaks in the foundation compromise the integrity of the entire home."[1]

AVOIDING THE SAND

If you've ever been to the beach, you know that the sand follows you long after you leave. It shows up in car seats, your hair, your clothes, and places you never expected it to be. Sand never stays contained. It spreads. It lingers long after you thought you left it behind.

A foundation of sand is the same. If you build a relationship on sin, it will spread into other areas and resurface where you least expect it.

Willow Creek Community Church had a promising beginning. Originally one of America's largest churches, many attributed Willow's success to its lead pastor, Bill Hybels. Hybels was a strong leader and skilled teacher. Whenever the founding story of Willow was shared, it revolved around the divine calling Hybels heard from God to start his church single-handedly, as well as his hard work to bring Willow to where it presently was. In essence, the foundation was based not on God's provision, but on Hybels'.

The church seemed to flourish for a long time, but the instability of its foundation eventually surfaced. Willow's true founding story was far different than the myth that was being told to its congregants. In Willow's early days, there was another founder of Willow, Dave Holmbo, who had resigned from his position after wrestling with a long history of sexual misconduct. Hybels and the elders kept Holmbo's behavior, as well as his role in starting Willow, secret from the rest of the church. Years later, in 2018, Hybels himself faced numerous allegations relating to sexual misconduct. Already on track to retire, he resigned early, walking away from the church he had supposedly raised single-handedly.

In short, Willow's *actual* foundation was built on two major weaknesses: the exaggerated status of Hybels and the covering up of sexual sin.

Mike Cosper, who researched this aspect of Willow's story, pointed out the power and fragility that founding myths like these can have.

> When you examine the Willow Creek story, you see how the identity of a church can be wrapped around one man and his vision . . . the elevation of the pastor to celebrity status, to essential status, as Hybels was, sets the table for disaster, institutionally and spiritually, if the leader falls.[2]

The cracks in Willow's foundation early on, and the choices made to avoid addressing them, ended up resurfacing and intensifying as the years wore on.

In the same way, your romantic foundation sets a precedent. What started a relationship is usually what it will slip back into. Put another way, the patterns that define your relationship at the beginning will be extremely difficult to get out of. I've seen this whenever I visit my parents. We have a healthy relationship, but when I stay with them long enough, our dynamic begins to drift back to the way it was when I was younger. When a foundation is set, it becomes the gravitational center of the relationship.

I know firsthand how bad foundations of sand can be. For many years, there was something wrong with how I dated women. My relationships would last a month or two until I ended them. Our interactions were fine, but something was missing. And then there was the anxiety, which began on the first date and only worsened as the relationship went on. I didn't look forward to spending time with them. If anything, I was incredibly stressed.

I recognized something was wrong and began evaluating the problem. Was it the quality of the women? No! The women I dated had a sincere relationship with God. Was it the relationship I had with them? No! We respected each other and didn't cross any boundaries. Was I afraid of commitment? No! I had been in relationships before where I felt completely okay. On paper, it made no sense why I was so stressed out. The relationships and the women were not the problem.

Eventually, I realized where the anxiety was coming from. The problem wasn't the women or the *way* I pursued them. It was the *reason* I pursued them in the first place. Every relationship where I felt anxious could be traced back to a moment in my life where I felt lonely or out of control. Every time I moved to a new state, started a new job, or struggled to find meaningful friendships, and I would compensate by seizing control over the only thing I could: my love life.

The foundation of my relationships was based not on Christ but on self-medication. I was pursuing women out of desperation, seeing them as a cure-all for my feelings of loneliness and lack of control. Each woman was a life preserver, not a lifelong companion. I dated women to escape feeling trapped, only to then feel trapped by the women I dated.

My love life was built on sand. The anxiety and stress I felt in singleness carried over into a foundation of anxiety and stress in dating. In the same way, unresolved sin can spread into the foundations we build our marriages upon. If you meet your future wife while cheating on your girlfriend, then when your marriage is at a low point you will feel the urge to find sexual gratification elsewhere. If you meet your future husband in hopes of finding validation in him, then when difficulties arise in your marriage you will feel a desire to find validation from your work, your children, or something else. If left unaddressed, sand spreads. Our emotional or spiritual problems, if ignored, cause incredible damage later down the road.

BUILDING ON THE ROCK

What, then, can we do? Foundations of sand are not always obvious, and if they're based in sin, how can we know we're building on rock instead? Also, what hope is there for couples whose marriage is already built on sand?

Once again, we can turn to Jesus for insight. Before his ministry even began, Jesus faced a temptation that threatened to compromise his foundation. Right after he was baptized, he went into the wilderness and fasted, and Satan came and tempted him. The first temptation targeted Jesus' hunger, the next his identity; but for the third, Satan aimed for Jesus' foundation.

> Again, the devil took him to a very high mountain and showed him all the kingdoms of the world and their glory. And he said to him, "All these I will give you, if you will fall down and worship me." Then Jesus said to him, "Be gone, Satan! For it is written, 'You shall worship the Lord your God and him only shall you serve.'"

(Matt. 4:8-10)

It seems ridiculous that Satan would offer Jesus, the Son of the Creator of the Universe, the world's kingdoms. And it is. But in laughing at the absurdity, we risk overlooking an important detail: Jesus was *tempted*. There was a part of him that struggled to resist Satan's offer.

Let's look at where Jesus was in this moment. He had just been baptized: his ministry hadn't started yet, and he had no disciples. He was about to walk down a long road, one that would end in unimaginable pain and death. Jesus knew what awaited him, and Satan was offering him the easy way out: a shortcut to success without the struggle or pain. If Jesus merely bowed to him, the kingdoms would be his.

But Satan offers this short-term solution at the long-term cost of Jesus' entire goal. If Jesus had bowed down to Satan, his ministry would be doomed before it ever began. His work, if he even did any, would be founded on Satan instead of God, on sand instead of rock. Jesus wasn't after the kingdoms of the world: he was seeking to establish *his* kingdom in the world. Despite the temptation, Jesus wasn't in a place of desperation. In the end, he was able to resist Satan's offer without budging from his foundation of rock. He knew that anything founded on a quick fix, rather than God's will, would crumble.

I am not Jesus, and when I try doing things solo, I always end up standing in sand. But, my failures are precisely why he saved me. In him and him alone, I am given a new foundation made of rock. Paul reminds us that "if anyone is in Christ, he is a new creation" (2 Cor. 5:17). If our stories were completely up to us, we would be drowning in quicksand. And yet, there is good news: we have a God who, through Christ, offers us a new foundation. A new story.

Not only does Christ save us from our foundations of sand, he himself *is* the foundation. "For no one can lay a foundation other than that which is laid, which is Jesus Christ" (1 Cor. 3:11). No other foundation is as infallible or as stable as Jesus. All else is sand.

In Jesus, you are not helpless in your circumstances. He gives you purpose and love beyond the baggage you carry or the wrongdoings you've committed. His redemption covers our sins, our shortcomings, and our founding stories.

In Jesus's parable of the prodigal son, the younger son squanders everything he has. He messes things up well beyond hope. But then, when he returns home, his father runs up and embraces him (Luke 15:20). The son, despite initially building his foundation on sand, is given a new foundation not because he found his own way out, but because he returned to his father.

BUILDING WITH GOD AS THE ARCHITECT

Rock is one the best building materials. It never rusts or decays, and its strength persists across thousands of years. If you build on the rock of Christ, he will do a work that extends far beyond your lifetime.

Many churches have rightly said that the gospel changes everything. When we not only hear Jesus' words but apply them, then how we live changes. How we date changes. How we pursue marriage changes. We don't act out of desperation, as though we are running out of time or possibilities. Instead, we walk in abundance, knowing that in Jesus we lack nothing. We have confidence in Christ, not only in his love for us, but in his plans for us, as well.

When we feel desperate, we are more likely to make compromises. Proverbs warns that "to one who is hungry everything bitter is sweet" (27:7). When we despair of finding our future spouse, we think having something less desirable is better than nothing at all. In our desperation, Satan can offer us the cute guy we're attracted to but know isn't right for us or the girl who says she loves Jesus but doesn't put her faith into action. We can end up making short-term choices that lead to long-term devastation.

If you aren't sure what foundation your life is built on, look at how you spend your time. Consider the "why" behind the choices you make or the emotions you feel. This isn't about micromanaging every detail of your life; it's about considering what your life and lifestyle point to. Where do you invest most of yourself? What does this say about you and your priorities? Do you spend most of your time watching sports, playing video games, or going to political rallies? Do you study scripture, pray, or spend time in church community?

We can say we want a godly person but live a life where we likely won't find them. If you desire a ministry-minded guy, you're likely not going to run into him at a bar or casino. If you seek a godly woman, chances are you won't run into her at a strip club. The founding story of your marriage is both about you and about your future spouse.

Right now, in your singleness, you have a say about what kind of foundation your future marriage will be established in. If God wills for you to be married, and you do so, and someone asks "How did you two meet?", will your story point to God? You can't control your future spouse's side, but you can control your own.

This isn't about controlling every outcome to find your idea of a perfect husband or wife. Don't reject a godly woman because you happened to run into her at a baseball game, or turn down a godly guy because he took you on a date that was less than perfect. Instead of focusing on orchestrating your love life, focus on reestablishing it in Christ.

It's easy to think we've messed up our lives and our singleness beyond the point of restoration. You might think that you're the furthest thing from a foundation of rock, that all your marriage will be is sand. But your story is still being written. If it's being written by you, your situation is indeed hopeless. But if you give God the pen, nothing will compare to the sentences he's writing.

Reflection Questions:

• Do you remember how your parents met, or how a couple you know found each other? What does that story say about their foundation, both good and bad? Can you see the fruits of that beginning in their relationship now?

• What have you built on a foundation of sand that later fell apart? How did the sand spread?

• What would you need to change about the way you live your life to have a founding story that points to Jesus? What beliefs or behaviors do you struggle to surrender to Jesus?

• What excites and frightens you about giving God the pen to write your story?

PART 2

LIFE AS A STRUGGLING ROMANTIC

7

THE COMPARISON GAME

The night before a friend's wedding, I was hanging out with him and some of the groomsmen when, as soon as the groom left the room, the conversation shifted. Several of the groomsmen were unmarried and lamented the fact that they were still single, using the occasion to call attention to their own loneliness.

"I'm never getting married!"

"Oh yeah? Well, *I've* never even been on a date."

"How come everyone is getting married before me?"

"No girl is *ever* going to like me."

I've thought those very sentences to myself, many times. However, it's one thing to feel lonely and quite another to take it out on others. It's detrimental. It's prideful. And it's indicative of a hidden poison affecting singles today.

Comparison is poisonous because, in small doses, it largely goes unnoticed. In our world today, we compare everything, from who wore it better to who did it faster to who is more popular, more successful, or more attractive. When comparison is present, even in less perceptible amounts, it impairs our ability to love ourselves, love others, and, most importantly of all, love God.

Comparison is a silent killer. It kills friendships, it kills contentment, and it kills our ability to celebrate the success of others. The dating scene is fraught with comparison. We measure how many dates we've been on, the compliments we received, and much more. Was he winking at me or at the girl behind me? Is she prettier? He's been on three dates this month, why can't I get one? Romance stops being a journey and becomes a competition. We see the same gender as romantic rivals and the opposite gender as menu options. We need to have their looks, their personality, their charm, convinced that would guarantee our success.

None of this is healthy. It draws our devotion away from God and turns it toward crushing the competition. Dating apps replace our devotionals, dates replace church services, and our significant other becomes our mission field. We don't focus on people, we focus on how close they get us toward the ideal marriage. We don't focus on love, we focus on results. We aren't becoming more like Jesus, we're becoming more envious and spiteful.

But many of us don't realize that the comparison game is rigged. No matter how we play, the strategy we employ, or the cards in our hands, we lose every time. When we compare ourselves to others, there are only two ways it can end: either I'm better than you, or you're better than me. If I conclude I'm better than you, I have an inflated view of myself. I see you as inferior and will likely treat you as such. On the other hand, if I conclude you're better than me, I will have a deflated view of myself. I will see the person God made me to be as inferior.

As struggling romantics, we can compare ourselves to other singles we view as competition and to those who look "happily married." But, the comparison game keeps going long after singleness ends. Comparison poisons the happiness married couples have with each other as well. If you are frustrated or disappointed with your spouse, you will start eyeing people to replace them or at least for your spouse to be more like.

You'll compare your marriage to others that seem better or happier somehow, encouraging discontentment to take root. There's always something to compare. Newlyweds are pressured to start producing children. First-time parents receive unwarranted feedback regarding their parenting choices and compare their children to others who seem better behaved. Then, they are asked when baby number two will happen. It never ends. As one married woman cautions:

> When you constantly compare your marriage to the seemingly perfect marriage next door, you're going to make yourself miserable. You'll never measure up to that mythical, blissful union. Instead of improving your own prospect for happiness, you'll sabotage your marriage.[1]

If we don't deal with comparison now as singles, it will continue to haunt us.

"WHAT IS THAT TO YOU?"

Does the Bible ever address comparison? Do you even need to ask? As a matter of fact, it shows up during a moment where the resurrected Jesus is sitting with his disciples. Jesus explains to Peter:

"When you were young, you used to dress yourself and walk wherever you wanted, but when you are old, you will stretch out your hands, and another will dress you and carry you where you do not want to go." (This he said to show by what kind of death he was to glorify God.) And after saying this he said to him, "Follow me."

(John 21:18-19)

Jesus is foreshadowing the death that Peter would eventually suffer, which tradition tells us was a crucifixion at the hands of the Romans. Even in these verses, Peter must have felt uneasy about this prophecy. He notices John sitting nearby and asks Jesus about him.

When Peter saw [John], he said to Jesus, "Lord, what about this man?" Jesus said to him, "If it is my will that he remain until I come, what is that to you? You follow me!"

(John 21:21-22)

We will never know the exact emotional state of Peter, but we can certainly understand his reaction. Jesus tells him something difficult, and his first response is to point to someone else and go "what about *him*?"

Can you think of a time when you felt like that? I definitely can. There have been countless occasions where a married couple will tell me a beautiful story about how they met, or a friend of mine finally goes on a date with someone who is an incredible fit for them, and in my heart, I wonder, "Lord, what about me?" I knew of a church leader who remarried, and a single man in the congregation privately lamented, "Why does *he* get to be married twice, and *I* still don't have anyone?"

It's the language of comparison. We throw ourselves between God and other people, wanting to know how we measure up. And yet, we need to hear Jesus asking, "What is that to you? You follow me." If someone gets married before you, what is that to you? If they are able to have children when you have not yet, what is that to you?

I don't see Jesus' question as derogatory. He's not saying, "What's wrong with you? Your relationship with me matters more than your petty problems." Rather, I see this question as him inviting us to look deeper into ourselves, at the "why" behind our pain. I see Jesus saying, "My dear child, why do you turn away from the exciting work I want to do in your life? I have a plan for you, but I can't tell you everything. Follow me and trust I have your best interests at heart."

Sometimes, comparison drives us to put conditions on our love for God. We barter with the Almighty, saying, "*If* you do this for me, *then* I will love you more." We say things like "if God loved me, he would give me a spouse by now" or "if God is so caring, why hasn't he blessed me with a family yet?" In essence, we conclude that God doesn't love us because he doesn't love us in the way we want him to.

When we compare ourselves to others, we signal that God's desire for us is not enough. When we aren't content with the body he gave us, the singleness he gave us, or the personality he gave us, we are implying that God's work is defective: a grim statement indeed. When we focus on obtaining instead of appreciating, God's goodness becomes defined by what he *should* do for us instead of what he's *already* done. When we restrict our appreciation of God's love, we see it less. Slowly, but inevitably, comparison impoverishes our lives—including our faith.

THE POISON OF ENVY

Jonathan should have wanted to kill David.

After all, his father did.

Saul was king over the Israelites, but his heart was becoming hardened. Since God made it clear that David was to inherit his kingdom, Saul wanted David dead, which forced David to become a fugitive. If there is anyone who should have been envious, it was Jonathan. As Saul's son and heir, Jonathan had every reason to want David dead, as well, so he could secure the throne—and the kingdom——for himself.

But Jonathan didn't. In fact, he remained one of David's closest friends, helping David avoid the clutches of Saul and escape. Jonathan said in his blessing over David, "May the Lord take vengeance on David's enemies" (1 Sam. 20:16). Jonathan not only kept David alive, he celebrated and supported David's calling to be king after Saul. When he could easily have been consumed with envy, Jonathan fully embraced where God wanted him, even if that place wasn't on a throne.

When comparison goes unchecked, it can lead to envy. I've encountered many struggling romantics who see the world through the perspective of envy and entitlement. When someone they know gets married or enters a serious relationship, they congratulate that person to their face and then complain behind their back. They spend their entire time at a wedding thinking that it should have been *them* at the altar instead. They act more like Saul than Jonathan.

I am no better. For a time in my life, I noticed I was developing a bitterness toward married couples. I was tired of reading books about singleness written by men and women who were married. I saw them as out-of-touch, as far removed. What could they know? What could they say to me that I couldn't figure out myself?

This prejudice affected how I felt toward married friends of mine. Sometimes they would text me when their wives had plans that night. They had some time to themselves and wondered if I would join them. Such a good friend! How thoughtful of them to reach out and think of me. But instead, I chose to see it as an indirect admission that they couldn't handle being alone for a night, something that I endured on a daily basis. Part of me thought, "Now you get it. Now you know the loneliness I feel. Eat it and weep."

I had legitimate feelings of frustration and loneliness, but comparing myself to married couples was creating an "us vs. them" mentality. I was developing envy toward people I loved because I was looking at how my happiness compared to theirs. Any attempt they made at friendship was viewed through bitterness. Envy is like a leak in the pipes of our feelings: if we're not careful, it spreads from the broken source and covers more of our lives.

Jesus says "By this all people will know that you are my disciples, if you have love for one another" (John 13:35). He doesn't say that by our love, *Christians* would know we are Jesus' disciples, he says *all people* will know. It is through our love for each other that both the Church and the world will see Jesus. Therefore, how we love one another is integral to our faith.

Comparison and envy restrict how we express love to each other. They convince us to see love through entitlement instead of unconditional service. One pastor points out that when you compare "you really want to succeed . . . but you also want everyone else to fail."[2] We shouldn't rejoice when our romantic rivals or fellow singles fail, but seek to love them as Christ loved us. As scripture reminds us, "Love . . . does not insist on its own way; it is not irritable or resentful; it does not rejoice at wrongdoing, but rejoices with the truth" (1 Cor. 13:4-6). Every time we fixate on the shortcomings of others and resent their successes, we become less loving.

THE TOXIN OF APPROVAL

If you have ever paid any attention to fashion trends, you know how fast they change. Every season brings a different color, a different look, a different must-have clothing item. If we try to stay on top of these trends, we'll never stop, because it never stops changing. People's approval is the same way: it's one of the driving forces behind comparison. If we aren't consumed by obtaining what others have, we're obsessed with winning their attention. But what people desire from you will constantly change. When we focus on winning over others, we distract ourselves from the stability of God's love.

Envying others is contrary to the heart of God. It prioritizes what others think of us versus what God thinks of us. If we focus on being noticed by others, we are unable to serve God. "For am I now seeking the approval of man, or of

God? Or am I trying to please man? If I were still trying to please man, I would not be a servant of Christ" (Gal. 1:10).

Instead of giving in to the endless game of approval-seeking and comparison-striving, Jesus calls us to follow him. It isn't about racing against other singles, it's about running toward him. Rather than rejoicing over the latest breakup or divorce or rejection, what would it look like to celebrate the victories of other singles? If we were turned down on a date, how could we respond graciously? If we experience a breakup, how can we embrace peace? We are called to bless those around us, including those who have what we want but still lack.

The same goes for those we might view as competitors. There have been two separate times in my life where another guy and I liked the same woman. Both times, I confided my feelings for a specific woman to a friend, and the friend confessed he liked her, too. How do you respond to something like that?

For me, I had to keep my hands open. For all we knew, the woman in question could prefer one of us or neither of us. We had to trust in God and not treat each other as rivals. Whatever happened would be God's will, the woman's will, or some combination of the two. The first time this happened, the other guy got the girl (though they later broke up), and the second time neither of us was successful. In both cases, however, the friendship I had with the guys remained intact.

Marriage isn't the finish line to a competition, and dating shouldn't be that way, either. Scripture is clear: marriage is a gift from God; therefore, God is the only one who can truly give it to us. There's no need to fight over a particular guy or girl. If God wills a relationship to work out between two people, it will. The gift of marriage isn't one we can force into our lives, and the more we try to do so, the weaker a foundation for that marriage we will build.

We need to walk in our singleness and dating relationships with open hands. I love what Job says, even in the midst of his suffering: "The Lord gave, and the Lord has taken away; blessed be the name of the Lord" (Job 1:21). This verse has become a daily prayer for me. We need to bless God when he gives *and* when he takes away. He knows what is good for us. When God blesses us, we often forget *he's* the one who provided the blessing. Then, when he takes something away, our prayers often sound like curses instead of blessings. We must praise God regardless of our present circumstances. Comparison is the thief of joy, and we need to find rest in the giver of joy.

THE ANTIDOTE OF THANKSGIVING

How do we find rest from comparison and envy and approval? By embracing contentment. When we get caught up in what we don't have, we lose sight of what God has already given. If we can't see how God currently provides for us, it will be harder to believe he will in the future. Therefore, the best way to minister to our hearts when envy threatens it is through thanksgiving. Paul affirms that "godliness with contentment is great gain" (1 Tim. 6:6). Peace permeates our lives when we acknowledge what God has provided, for in "whatever you do, in word or deed, do everything in the name of the Lord Jesus, giving thanks to

God the Father through him" (Col. 3:17). Contentedness is far from easy, especially when everything around us revolves around comparison. Reasons to feel "behind" in life will readily and reliably present themselves, but reasons for gratitude have to be consciously sought out and dwelt upon.

Comparison never ends. There will always be men or women who appear more attractive, more desirable, and more successful than you are. Contentedness isn't something you stumble into—it's something you have to seek out. To be content is to be countercultural. It isn't limited to moments where everything is going right or the last week of November. It applies to *every* season. Whether homeless, nationless, landless, spouseless, or childless, Christians from all walks of life can praise God for what he's done in their lives.

Look at your life and try to find reasons to praise God, and I promise you'll be surprised by how many blessings he has already provided: whether it's income, a roof over your head, friends, or something as simple as breathing or having food to eat when you're hungry. You'll find that God has already given you much. Giving thanks will sustain you throughout your future marriage, as well.

The world doesn't need more miserable singles: we already have plenty of those. What the world is sorely missing are singles whose attitude reflects that of Christ, unburdened and full of peace. When we dwell on the blessings of God, we become a blessing to others and enjoy the journey we're on so much more.

Reflection Questions:

• Who or what do you often compare yourself to? Is there someone or something you wish you had in your life but don't?

• Have you felt like you deserved certain outcomes or blessings because of your behavior or faithfulness?

• What are the biggest blessings God has already given you? What do you have in your life that you are thankful for?

8

HOW TO BE ATTRACTIVE

Years ago, my brother Josh and I were on our way to spend a weekend with family in Wisconsin. At some point, we needed to stop for food, and Josh recommended a fast food place that supposedly had good root beer.

We walked in, where a girl at the front took our order. As we waited for our food to arrive, Josh left for the bathroom. I sat alone, anticipating the savory root beer, when the same girl who took our order arrived with the food. As she set it all down, she said to me in a whisper, "You're very cute. If you'd like to hang out sometime . . ." and placed a sticky note on the table with her name and phone number.

I was baffled. I was wearing shorts, a T-shirt, and my glasses. My attire was for a road trip, not for impressing anyone. The last thing I expected was for someone to make a move on me, especially when I didn't put any effort into my appearance.

Maybe it was the root beer.

Whether on a date or in a fast food restaurant, our culture prioritizes appearance. You have likely heard that "looks aren't everything". It's a sweet sentiment, until you look around. Scantly-clad models adorn the covers of magazines, painted with expensive makeup and photoshopped into perfection. On dating apps, the first thing that greets you on someone's profile is a photo of them. From art to advertising, YouTube thumbnails to Instagram filters, our culture is overrun by images of people designed to look as appealing as possible. Looks aren't everything, but everything around us seems to say the exact opposite.

Some people go to extreme lengths to look good. Actors who play superheroes go through incredibly rigorous exercise regimens and nutrition plans that are unsustainable in the long-term. Hugh Jackman dehydrated himself for 36 hours before filming in order to make his muscles pop in shirtless scenes. It takes about 100 hours to die from dehydration.[1]

Unhealthiness is prevalent at the local level, too. Men often compromise their personalities to appeal to women. This is true with the majority of male-oriented online classes and "alpha male" culture, which wrongly teach that hyper-confidence, aggression, and emotional manipulation can make you romantically irresistible. Women, on the other hand, often compromise their physical appearance to appeal to men. Whether in the clothes they wear or the latest makeup trends, there's a sense that if you don't conform, you won't be accepted. This even affects preteen girls, many of whom buy skincare products they see on social media. The products—intended for adults—end up giving many of them long-lasting blisters and severe allergic reactions.[2] Looking good isn't just a priority: we are destroying ourselves to do it.

How we are seen by others matters deeply to us, but desirability is hard to measure. So, we often turn to external factors: how many likes we get on our selfies, how many matches we get on dating apps, or how many heads turn when we wear a certain outfit. We can settle for dating someone who isn't the best because we think "I'll never score someone this good-looking ever again."

Many churches acknowledge that attraction is important in dating, but don't spend much time on the topic otherwise. This is a shame, because the Bible not only has much to say about attraction, but offers a deeper understanding of how we can navigate it.

SEXY AND YOU (DON'T) KNOW IT

"Being attractive" is usually seen as something you have or something you don't. You're either attractive or unattractive, a beautiful swan or an ugly duckling, with not much room in-between. There are rare moments where a transformation can occur, either by a "glow-up" or by dedicating yourself to the gym, but aside from those moments your attraction level is seen as objectively unchangeable. However, as we'll explore shortly, being attractive is partially objective, partially subjective. There are elements we can't control, and elements that we have more control over than we expect.

The objective aspects of attraction are obvious. Your physical appearance will look pretty much the same. You cannot get a completely new face, voice, body type, or height. Age isn't reversible, either. There are surgeries and procedures which offer some modification, but you still cannot become a totally different human being. Simply put, you look the way you look.

This is often where our understanding of attraction ends. We recognize our body is a highly visible, barely-changeable aspect of who we are, so we analyze our physical appearances, taking stock of every imperfection, and use our findings to determine people we have a shot at dating versus people who are "out of our league". We fixate on what we cannot control and often despair as a result. We determine our desirability based solely on how we look.

There are several problems with this approach. For one, while our bodies remain basically the same, our opinion of them does not. Some days I'll wake up, look in the mirror, and think I look like Jabba the Hutt's cousin. Then, I'll go to the gym and do three pushups and return to the mirror now convinced I look like hot stuff (even though my body has hardly changed). If we assess our desirability based solely on our opinions, we will never be consistently happy.

Another danger is that we are our own worst critic. If we look for imperfections, we will always find something wrong. In your eyes, you will never look good enough, no matter how often you work out or how well you apply your makeup or what hygiene products you buy. While our bodies remain objectively the same, we do not (and, I believe, cannot) objectively evaluate our bodies.

We care about physical imperfections because we think they keep others from loving us. Yet, when we look at ourselves, we do not know if what we see is exactly what others see. In fact, it isn't. We can't control how others will see us. We can't even control whether people are attracted to us or not! As Matt Lantz observes, someone might be attracted to a part of us that we weren't expecting.

> Anything from our eye color to our athletic build can be a "trigger" that someone else finds attractive. The problem is we just don't know what those triggers are for everybody

else. Often times a quality or characteristic that we consider to be our most attractive feature is not what creates the spark for someone else.[3]

Our objective appearance isn't as bad as we might believe. Just because we think our body is unattractive doesn't mean someone else will think the same thing. As Matt mentioned, what people desire in you will likely be different than what you believe your most attractive features are.

You might worry that your weight is the only thing keeping you from finding a spouse, when it might be the very thing that draws their eye to you in the first place. You might be insecure about your height, your muscle mass, your personality, or your laugh, when those exact traits might make you irresistible to someone else. I might think I look like a dumpster with legs, but someone across the room may be distracted by how handsome I look. There might be a girl with no makeup and a messy hair bun who thinks she looks awful, but I may find her stunning.

Some guys prefer shorter women, while some prefer taller. Some women don't mind a dad bod, while others prefer someone who actively works out. While it's impossible for everyone in the world to find you physically attractive, someone out there will. There is no such thing as being universally attractive or unattractive. Clearly, when it comes to being desirable, there's more than meets the eye.

THE FACTOR OF CHARACTER

There was a guy whom I will call Brett. Brett had been single for a while and, boy, if you had any doubts Brett was single, wait until he started talking. He would constantly mention how ugly he thought he was, complain about how unfair his love life had been, and bemoan that he would never find that special someone.

As blunt and pessimistic as Brett was, I think there's something we can relate to in what he says. You might never say it out loud, but maybe you repeat the same things to yourself. You look in the mirror and call yourself unattractive. You glance at someone you feel is a romantic rival and you envy how they look, how everyone seems to love them, and how easily they get into relationships.

The thing about Brett, however, was that his lifestyle was filled with bad habits. His diet consisted exclusively of unhealthy food. His living space was a constant mess. He would often procrastinate on work. He frequently compared himself to others and was hard on himself whenever he made mistakes. He struggled with low self-esteem, and his insecurities were especially prominent when he was around women.

The problem with Brett had nothing to do with his looks. In fact, he looked quite normal. Ironically, Brett *was* unattractive, but it wasn't in the way he thought. He wasn't *physically* unattractive—he was *acting* unattractive. The problem wasn't with his face, it was with his character.

Many single people, especially women, lament their looks. "I know that looks aren't everything, but they're necessary for a guy to talk to me in the first place!" Looks might help get you a first date, but if you're a terrible person underneath, you won't get a second. You can find a girlfriend or boyfriend, but you won't be able to keep them.

Character matters more than looks. There have been times where I've encountered a woman who was incredibly physically attractive. As soon as we struck up a conversation, however, I quickly discovered that while she was pleasing to look at, her personality was another story. Despite the woman's appearance remaining the same, her unattractive character changed how I felt toward her. On the other hand, there have been women who weren't the most attractive person I'd ever seen, but as I got to know their heart, they actually became more desirable in my eyes.

The Old Testament gives us a better understanding of character. Israel begs God for a king and he gives them Saul, a man described as good-looking: "There was not a man among the people of Israel more handsome than he. From his shoulders upward he was taller than any of the people" (1 Sam. 9:2). But despite his impressive physique, Saul's heart begins to drift from God. Soon, God sends the prophet Samuel to find Saul's successor.

God tells Samuel that one of Jesse's sons will be king. One of his sons immediately stands out to Samuel. "[Samuel] looked on Eliab and thought, 'Surely the Lord's anointed is before him'" (1 Sam. 16:6). Eliab bears much of the same attributes Saul has: he's handsome and has a mighty appearance.

Samuel is impressed. "But the Lord said to Samuel, 'Do not look on [Eliab's] appearance or on the height of his stature, because I have rejected him. For the Lord sees not as man sees: man looks on the outward appearance, but the Lord looks on the heart'" (1 Sam. 16:7).

The Bible is not against good looks, nor is it against keeping a healthy body, but those attributes are nowhere near as important as what's in our hearts: the quality of our relationship with Jesus. Paul clarifies that "while bodily training is of some value, godliness is of value in every way, as it holds promise for the present life and also for the life to come" (1 Tim. 4:8).

There is nothing inherently wrong with wearing makeup or maintaining a pleasing appearance. It's not bad to be physically attracted to someone, but it shouldn't be all you focus on. If she tells you she's "spiritual, but not religious" or he encourages you to push your boundaries beyond what you're comfortable with, do you ignore them because they look good? Or do you stand your ground?

Even if your body looks fantastic, looks diminish over time —the body you have in your twenties won't be the same as it will in your forties—and alter egos attract people to a false image of you, rather than the real you. In either case, they distract from what really matters. God doesn't weigh the physical appearance, he weighs the heart, and as followers of Jesus, we should seek to do the same.

SEEING OUR VALUE

Scripture says, "As in water face reflects face, so the heart of man reflects the man" (Prov. 27:19). The most attractive we can be is when we align our character with Christ's: not for the sake of finding a spouse or winning someone over, but for the sake of our relationship with him. Truly being attractive means accepting that Christ loves you, instead of striving to make others love you.

Proverbs also tells us, "Charm is deceitful, and beauty is vain, but a woman who fears the Lord is to be praised" (31:30). Men who focus on being as charming as possible will either become someone they aren't or become exhausted by maintaining the act. Women who fixate on physical flawlessness will become undone either by a small fault in their body or by the inevitability of aging. But, for the Christian, we have a greater security in the love and approval God has already given us, as well as the bodies and personalities he has made us with.

When we ask ourselves "am I attractive?", what we're typically asking is really "am I desirable in the eyes of desirable people?" We are all drawn to what we desire. People who don't have a relationship with Christ are drawn to themselves, but those who love Christ will be drawn to those whose hearts remind them of his.

The closer you get to God, the more you'll love what he loves and desire what he desires. Your character will start to reflect his character. When you become more like Christ, you will attract those who desire his character as well. When we realize we are already valued and made worthy by God, our actions reflect that value and worthiness. When we find ourselves being pursued by the Creator of the Universe, we don't find ourselves chasing desperately after others.

Handsome or not, beautiful or not, looks are not what ultimately matter. They have some value, but not *ultimate* value. David tells God, "I praise you, for I am fearfully and wonderfully made" (Ps. 139:14). You were deliberately crafted by God, from your body shape to the length of your limbs to the dimples in your smile to the color of your eyes.

He knew what he was doing when he made you, and in his eyes you are beautiful.

God accepts and loves you as you are, and if you find a spouse whose heart reflects God's, they will echo the same thing.

Reflection Questions:

• What physical expectations or beauty standards in our culture feel the most unrealistic?

• Have you struggled with your appearance in the past? Do you still? Where does that insecurity come from?

• What does godly character look like to you? What would it look like in someone you date or marry?

9

TAMING THE WORKHORSE

In our culture, we define ourselves by the work we do.

I saw this in a weekly Bible study I led. One of our members put more effort into serving and volunteering than anyone else. Whenever we began to plan something or organize an event, she would work ahead before we had made any official plans. By the time we met the following week, she would bombard us with her ideas, research, and the names of people she had already reached out to.

On its own this wasn't bad—if maybe overwhelming at times—but whenever those plans would change or when we didn't work as hard as she did, she became angry. Because she kept setting the bar beyond what anyone else could do, she became bitter, using her work as a standard to compare the rest of us to. She resented us when we didn't work at her level. Because she overexerted herself and rest of us didn't, she thought no one else cared as much as she did. Without realizing it, she was prioritizing her love of ministry over her love of God.

It is so easy to find worth in our work. Everything around us, whether in school, online, or in the workplace, seems to push us toward less sleep and more productivity. The world of dating has become a hustle in its own right, as optimization has become the focal point of dating apps. We have less time to spend, so if we meet someone, we need to quickly assess if they're a fit because otherwise we're wasting our time not swiping on other people. If we aren't satisfied with our matches, we retool our dating profile in the hopes of better results. The line between work and love has become blurred.

The freedom and flexibility that makes singleness a blessing can also make it a curse, allowing us to push ourselves to work longer and harder, without a spouse or children to keep our schedules in check and remind us to make room for relationships. If we are not giving ourselves to the pursuit of relationships, we're likely pursuing professional achievement instead.

WORKING HARD

As singles, we are particularly susceptible to being overworked. I learned this after starting my first singles group. We were going through a book which mentioned the exploitation of singles in the workplace. At the time, I had just started my first job out of college, and wasn't sure how applicable this idea still was to singles in my generation. Surely, in our growing understanding of work-life balance, we've matured in this area as a society.

But when we discussed this chapter, I was shocked at how many singles still experienced this. I heard many stories where people were pushed to work overtime solely *because* they were single. One single who was working in ministry had a supervisor who said to him, half-jokingly, "It'll be a shame once you get married and have kids: I won't be able to keep you here all day anymore."

However, our tendency to be overworked goes beyond our bosses: we can push *ourselves* to work long hours, as well. We put in extra hours, learn new skills, and pad out our resumés because we have the time and capability to do so.

There is nothing wrong with work itself. In fact, as Christians, we are to work like no one else. "Whatever you do, work heartily, as for the Lord and not for men, knowing that from the Lord you will receive the inheritance as your reward. You are serving the Lord Christ" (Col. 3:23-24). We are to work heartily—some translations say "enthusiastically" —so our hearts should be in what we do. And yet, our motivation for doing so distinguishes us. We aren't working for God's approval, for we already have it (2 Tim. 2:15). We are working *out* of approval, working as if serving God himself. As Peter Scazzero notes, "Many of us know the experience of being approved for what we do. Few of us know the experience of being loved for being just who we are."[1]

Whatever our job is, whether blue-collar or white-collar, dream job or worst-case scenario, retail or entrepreneurship, we do it all as if doing it for God himself. My dad demonstrated this principle while he was a college student. He got a job as a bus driver, shuttling other people around the campus. It was a fairly straightforward job: drive the bus from point A to point B, then back to point A, then repeat. It wasn't my dad's dream job—far from it—but that didn't stop him from wanting to bring his best. He made a mental note of the potholes along his route so he could drive around them, making the rides smoother and more enjoyable.

He was also very creative, and wondered how he could bring that into what he did. He decided to make some of his bus rides themed. One day, he dressed up as a pilot, treating the bus like an airplane flight. Other times, he held trivia contests, giving the passengers questions to figure out. And people noticed. He ended up in the college newspaper for his work. People became excited to ride the bus because of his investment in a job many took for granted. Dad didn't feel called to be a bus driver, but instead of reserving his gifts for work he was passionate about, he brought passion into the work he was already doing.

We see a similar relationship with work in the book of Daniel. Both Daniel and his friends were forced from their homeland (and from their families) into a pagan empire. Although they lived in a nation with different cultural and religious beliefs, Daniel and his friends worked hard to invest in where they were. They not only rose to the top of their class but were more distinguished than those who were already working for the king (Daniel 1:17-20).

And yet, both Daniel and his friends continuously faced situations where they had to choose between God or their career. While training under the Chaldeans, Daniel asked to self-impose a dietary restriction out of respect for God's law (Daniel 1:8). Despite Daniel not having any political leverage or authority, his request was honored. Daniel's friends, Hananiah, Mishael, and Azariah (you may know them as Shadrach, Meshach, and Abednego) openly refused to bow down to the king's golden statue, despite knowing it would result in them being thrown into a fiery furnace and killed (Daniel 3:8-12).

Daniel and his friends placed God above everything else, including their careers. As struggling romantics, we are called to do the same. It can be tempting to find worth in what we do, to work overtime to make more money or climb the corporate ladder. But, like our desire for marriage, our faith informs how we perceive and engage in our jobs. Work is an important part of our life, but it is not the source of our life: God is.

HARDLY WORKING

Not only are we called to work like no one else, but we are also called to rest like no one else. People smarter than I have pointed out that we are human *beings*, not human *doings*. We are not meant to be *doing* stuff all the time. Rest is essential for us. But what does this look like for our faith? If we are to work like no one else and rest like no one else, this can understandably seem paradoxical. Paul clarifies that we are "created in Christ Jesus for good works, which God prepared beforehand, that we should walk in them" (Eph. 2:10). The saving work has already been done in Christ, and the work we are presently called to do has been prepared for us in advance by God.

Jesus alludes to this when he says, "my yoke is easy, and my burden is light" (Matt. 11:30). A yoke was hand-crafted to fit around the neck of an oxen: it was meant to fit well. The works God has planned are designed with us in mind and are well within our ability to carry out.

This work/rest relationship is demonstrated in the story of Mary and Martha. Mary sits at Jesus' feet and listens to his words while Martha is "distracted with much serving" (Luke 10:40). Martha complains to Jesus about her sister, wanting Mary to help her. But Jesus replies, "Martha, Martha, you are anxious and troubled about many things, but one thing is necessary. Mary has chosen the good portion, which will not be taken away from her" (Luke 10:41-42).

I've heard lots of sermons that bash Martha. "Wow, look at her! So lost in meaningless work when Jesus is right there." But did you pay attention to the verses? Martha was serving. The work she did was *good*, but it was distracting her from Christ. We see this in Jesus' response to her: he doesn't criticize *what* Martha is doing, but *why* and *when*. He sees her anxiety and mental occupation. She was so wrapped up in *doing* that she couldn't focus on *being* with Jesus. In other words, she wasn't working from a place of rest but a place of stress. And stress almost made her miss Jesus, who was right in front of her.

When we serve God, whether at work or in church, we must be careful (especially in our work-centric culture) not to wrap up our worth in what we do. If we hold our career ambitions, our job title, or our industry reputation too tightly, we become anxious, stressed, and distracted from the presence of God.

As struggling romantics, we need to recognize that rest isn't just necessary for our own health, it is fundamental in connecting with other people. When we're overworked and distracted, it affects our capacity for relationship. Busyness affects our presence. We can remain distracted by work even on the weekends or vacation. If we're occupied all the time, either physically or mentally, we won't have room for friends, romantic relationships, or Jesus. As Jefferson Bethke points out, "you can't love someone when you are hustling. And you can't love someone when you're going fast. (Just ask my kids if I'm loving them well when I try to get out the door in two seconds when we are late.)"[2] If we desire a spouse or children someday, we need to consider what sacrifices in our our professional and ministerial lives those relationships will demand.

We can also use busyness as an excuse to avoid our commitments to people. Maybe your small group is going out to serve somewhere, and that isn't your thing. Maybe your friend wants to talk to you about something difficult, and you're scared how the conversation will go. Maybe you feel convicted to spend more time with God, but the demands of your job scream louder than the Holy Spirit does, and you convince yourself you'll get around to God once things quiet down at work. We allow work to dictate our commitments.

When we rest, we are able to be present, and Jesus modeled presence well. He was incredibly generous with his time, and engaged with disruptions instead of impatiently brushing them aside. At one point, Jesus is following a man whose daughter is dying. Time is of the essence. Then, a woman who had been suffering from a disease touches Jesus as he passes by, and she is healed. Immediately, Jesus stops to find who touched him, and listens to the woman as she shares her story (Mark 5:32-34). There is no reason for him to stop for her: she has already been healed. Yet, Jesus takes time to connect with the woman.

Practicing presence is about making space for God and others. Sometimes, when I'm driving, I'll use the silence to pray instead of listening to music or podcasts. Sometimes, I'll say "yes" to spontaneous moments with friends and community. Other times, when I'm worn out, I'll say "no" so I can be more present for future interactions. When we work like no one else and rest like no one else, we will then be able to love like no one else. We will delight in our work without being held captive by it.

Jesus says, "Come to me, all who labor and are heavy laden, and I will give you rest" (Matt. 11:28). Going on a vacation with friends might be somewhat restful, but it isn't always affordable. Jesus offers us a rest that is not only freely and constantly available, but one that can give you a peace that no vacation can do. As the author of Hebrews urges us, "there remains a Sabbath rest for the people of God, for whoever has entered God's rest has also rested from his works as God did from his. Let us therefore strive to enter that rest" (Heb. 4:9-11).

WORKING HEARTILY

There's a danger for us to interpret "work like no one else" as "work harder than everyone else", where we never take our eyes off the next step. Working hard doesn't necessarily mean working well. Working well *involves* working hard, but not all who work hard work well. You can stay overtime, push yourself beyond your limits, and pour hours into your career, but if you don't keep Christ at the center, it will all be for nothing.

Let not the wise man boast in his wisdom, let not the mighty man boast in his might, let not the rich man boast in his riches, but let him who boasts boast in this, that he understands and knows me . . .

(Jer. 9:23-24)

Your success, wealth, or wisdom is secondary to knowing God. You can say to yourself, "I'm not as smart as so-and-so" or "I'm not as successful as so-and-so," but those metrics aren't what's important. As Jesus warns us, "Do not lay up for yourselves treasures on earth . . . but lay up for yourselves treasures in heaven, where neither moth nor rust destroys and where thieves do not break in and steal. For where your treasure is, there your heart will be also" (Matt. 6:19-21). Where do you have the most treasure stored up? If you place your value in the money and career you have, you will never have enough, for "he who loves money will not be satisfied with money, nor he who loves wealth with his income; this also is vanity" (Ecc. 5:10).

I saw this with a colleague who, after freelancing for years, finally got a job with this small company he always wanted to work for. I sent him a message congratulating him. In response, he said, "Thanks! I'm excited, as well. Hopefully, this will bolster my resumé for a bigger company I'm looking at." Days after landing a great job opportunity, he was already looking at the next one.

As Christians, we are to *bless* the world. "Commit your work to the Lord, and your plans will be established" (Prov. 16:3). We shouldn't perpetually focus on getting the next promotion or the perfect career, but dedicate whatever work we have to God's purposes and the blessing of others. This might look like taking a coworker's shift, or simply coming to work with a smile and asking how someone's day is. Maybe it looks like pretending your bus route is an airline. Maybe it's serving more at your local church. Maybe it's serving *less* at your church. Maybe it's turning down a promotion to ensure you have space for relationships in your life. If we, as singles, worked to bless others, then lives would change. The *world* would change.

Whatever you can do, do it. God isn't discouraged by your limitations. He won't give up on you because of your medical issues, low mental health, or minimum-wage job. Whatever you have to give, give it, even if it's only a penny (Luke 21:1-14). When you do work to glorify God, whatever it may be, the world will be blessed as a result.

Reflection Questions:

• We are to work like no one else, rest like no one else, and love like no one else. Which of these three do you struggle to live out the most? What prevents you from doing so?

• Do you have enough room in your life for meaningful relationships? Why or why not? How could you start to prioritize presence more than productivity?

• Read Hebrews 10:24. How can you love those around you and stir them up to do good works? How could you use your singleness to do this? How could you do this at work?

10

FRIENDS WANTED

Loneliness has become an epidemic. Literally.

Across the world, affecting all ethnicities and ages, rates of social isolation have gone up. According to a report by Gallup and Meta, which covered over 140 countries, one in four young people feels lonely.[1] In fact, loneliness has become such a prominent problem that the World Health Organization labeled it a global health concern and, in 2023, launched a commission to begin finding solutions.[2] One reporter, who analyzed loneliness over America's last few decades, was alarmed by his findings. He concluded, "In short, there is no statistical record of any other period in U.S. history when people have spent more time on their own."[3]

Why are we more isolated than ever before? Is it the prevalence of social media? Working too many hours a day? Those darn smartphones? Professionals and armchair experts, alike, have debated the exact causes, but everyone agrees that the effects of this isolation are concerning.

It doesn't take statistics to state the obvious: we were made to live life with others. But this can be tricky to understand because people, in and of themselves, can't fix loneliness. You can be in a room full of people and still feel like something is missing. If anything, crowds can make you feel *more* lonely. This doesn't mean isolating is okay, it means there is a key component in our relationship with others that's missing. The symptoms can be subtle, like an itchy sweater: if you move around and keep busy, it's harder to detect, but as soon as you sit still, the itchiness returns until it feels impossible to ignore.

It's not the *quantity* of people that resolves loneliness, it's the *quality* of our relationships with them. It isn't about whether we know people, but whether we are known by people. Just like physical pain reminds us we need bodily healing, loneliness is an emotional pain that reminds us we need deep friendships.

FINDING FRIENDSHIPS

My first two friendships came out of nowhere. I was in the third grade when I joined a new school and immediately felt out-of-place. I didn't know anyone. On the first day of school, my teacher introduced me to the rest of the class. "Everyone, this is Daniel. He is new to our school. Would anyone like to show him around during recess?"

I didn't think anyone would bother. After all, they had all known each other since kindergarten (which, in elementary school years, basically meant they were lifelong friends). But almost immediately, a hand shot up. A boy in my class took me under his wing and enthusiastically showed me around. We discovered we had a lot in common: namely, that we both liked Star Wars. That is how I made my first friend.

Several weeks later, I was running through the playground when a kid suddenly fell from the sky, wiping out on the wood chips in front of me. He had been attempting to climb the monkey bars and slipped. I asked him if he was okay. Completely unfazed, he said he was. That is how I made my second friend.

Neither friendship happened in a way I could have expected, much less planned for. And yet, there was something about the way our lives effortlessly came together that felt like it was meant to be. Did I choose my friends? Yes and no. Friends are not something we can single-handedly bring about ourselves. Ultimately, it is God who brings friends together. C.S. Lewis remarks on this:

> . . . in Friendship . . . we think we have chosen our peers. In reality, a few years' difference in the dates of our births, a few more miles between certain houses, the choice of one university instead of another . . . the accident of a topic being raised or not raised at a first meeting—any of these chances might have kept us apart. But, for a Christian, there are, strictly speaking, no chances. A secret Master of the Ceremonies has been at work. Christ, who said to the disciples, 'Ye have not chosen me, but I have chosen you,' [John 15:16] can truly say to every group of Christian friends, 'You have not chosen one another but I have chosen you for one another.'[4]

To put it another way, friends don't choose the friendship, the friendship chooses them. Friends discover each other as a result of God's orchestration.

This truth can seem counterintuitive, especially in discussing loneliness. If God is the force behind friendship, what hope do we have in escaping loneliness? But our hope is only valid if God understands and loves friendship, which he does.

The Bible emphasizes the importance of relationships, from God providing Adam with Eve in Genesis (Gen. 2:23) to our communion with each other and God, uninhibited by sin in the final pages of Revelation (Rev. 21:3). It's also full of friendship. In Exodus, Aaron and Hur helped Moses hold up his staff so the Israelites could claim victory (Ex. 17:10-13). Jonathan protected David from his father, the king, who sought to kill him (1 Sam. 19:1-2). Ruth insisted on staying by the side of her mother-in-law Naomi, even though it meant moving to a foreign country (Ruth 1:16-18).

God's love of friendship is even more prominent in Jesus, who says that we, his followers, are his friends (John 15:15). God does more than champion friendship—he *is* friendship. As a Trinity, three distinct persons in one, God exists in and is community. He wants friendship for us because, since we were made in his image, we cannot fully reflect God if we do not exist in community. Just as he himself wants a close and personal connection with you, God also desires to join you to others with whom you can enjoy a close and personal connection—and not just in marriage.

INTERDEPENDENT FRIENDSHIPS

God created us for friendships and brings people into our lives. But what does friendship look like, practically, for us here on earth? In a world of sinful people, friendship can be twisted in all sorts of ways. We can befriend people who want a relationship with us too much, or those who don't want it enough. In other words, we encounter those who are too dependent on us and those too independent from us.

Here, scripture paints a picture not of dependence nor independence, but of interdependence. Stephen R. Covey, in his famous book *The 7 Habits of Highly Effective People*, describes these concepts: "Dependent people need others to get what they want. Independent people can get what they want through their own effort. Interdependent people combine their own efforts with the efforts of others to achieve their greatest success."[5] Dependent people can't function on their own. Independent people aren't able to rely on others. When we interdepend on one another, we combine our strengths and cover each other's weaknesses. This interdependence is God's design for human relationships.

For this reason, "two are better than one, because they have a good reward for their toil. For if they fall, one will lift up his fellow. But woe to him who is alone when he falls and has not another to lift him up!" (Ecc. 4:9-10). Friendships based in dependence or independence are one-sided: if one person falls down, the other can't be counted on to lift them up. One of you will primarily provide support and empathy more than the other. Neither of these relationships are true friendships.

Interdependence, on the other hand, is two-sided and built on mutual reliance. We are to "bear one another's burdens" (Gal. 6:2) which means being both capable of handling someone else's burdens and being vulnerable enough to trust others with yours.

It is this interdependence that makes up the Body of Christ: depending upon one another, as well as being individuals who can be depended on. The author of Hebrews describes this as such: "let us consider how to stir up one another to love and good works, not neglecting to meet together, as is the habit of some, but encouraging one another, and all the more as you see the Day drawing near" (Heb. 10:24-25). We cannot experience the body of Christ alone. As Jesus says, "where two or three are gathered in my name, there am I among them" (Matt. 18:20). This also means we cannot do the Christian life alone. We were made to live in tandem with others.

INFLUENTIAL FRIENDSHIPS

In college, I joined a friend group where gossip played a major role. Whenever someone in the group liked someone else, or when there was drama, everyone would know about it except for the person it was about. Over time, I realized the effect this had on me. The more time I spent in close proximity to them, the more of a gossip I was. In other words, my friends shaped the person I was becoming.

When we depend on each other, we also influence one other. "Iron sharpens iron, and one man sharpens another" (Prov. 27:17). This is necessary for friendships, that we shape and sharpen each other. But we also need to be aware who we are being sharpened into. Scripture warns: "Whoever walks with the wise becomes wise, but the companion of fools will suffer harm" (Prov. 13:20). As the saying goes, "show me your friends, and I'll show you your future."

The people you are closest to will have the strongest influence on the person you become. This doesn't mean we don't associate with sinners—Jesus did—but it means we engage with them differently than we do with our fellow brothers and sisters in Christ. We must be wise in understanding the difference between having compassion for someone who doesn't know the Gospel and giving that person an influential voice in our lives. It's one thing to befriend a nonbeliever. It's another to allow their priorities and their heart to affect yours.

As struggling romantics, this is also why we must be thoughtful in considering who we marry. If those who are closest to you have the greatest say in who you become, then no one will influence you more than your spouse. They will be the person you see at the beginning and end of your day, the person with whom you share your heart, your dreams, and your shortcomings. They will know you on a level that no one else will. Therefore, they will be able to encourage you like no one else, and they will be able to hurt you like no one else. This is why King Solomon, despite being the wisest man who ever lived, turned away from God: because of his wives, who didn't have a relationship with God (1 Kings 11:1-8, Neh. 13:26).

Look at your life right now. When a friend compliments you, it's reassuring. But when a person you have a crush on compliments you, their words make your entire day. When you date someone, you are setting them on a path that will result in them becoming the closest, most influential friend you have. So, if you want to do romance right, you have to do friendship right first.

If you don't know what healthy, biblical friendship looks like, you won't know what to look for in a healthy, biblical marriage. This can be confusing, as we don't often see friendship as something compatible with dating or romance. Typically, when someone you're interested in says they "want to be friends," it means the door to future marriage is closing instead of opening! While friendship isn't the sole ingredient in marriage, it's an integral part of the foundation. As Pastor Timothy Keller explains, "Marriage is not basically romance garnished with friendship, it is basically friendship garnished with romance."[6]

I am not trying to imply that Christian couples should be friends first before they start dating. It is possible to develop a friendship along with the relationship, but doing so will be far more difficult if you don't know what healthy friendship looks like. If we have friends who empathize deeply with us, we will seek a spouse who empathizes in a similar way. If we struggle to receive feedback graciously from our friends, we will struggle when our spouse delivers criticism. If we avoid confronting friends about the areas in their life that concern us, we will avoid doing the same in our marriage.

Biblical friendship is sacrificial. "Love one another with brotherly affection. Outdo one another in showing honor" (Rom. 12:10). Granted, the affection you show your spouse will be different than the affection you would show a sibling, but the mandate to love, serve, and honor each other carries over into marriage. Do you want to be the best spouse you can be? Then start by being the best friend you can be.

DATING & FRIENDSHIPS

Friendships don't just provide us with examples of *who* to date, they also give us a community that we can lean on *as* we date. Sadly, as comedian Trevor Noah has argued, isolation has had an adverse effect on our romantic relationships as well.

We shouldn't take for granted how much the abandoning or the ignoring of friendships has affected romantic relationships, because people have now shifted all of the expectation, all of the support, all of the love that they got from a community of friends, and they have moved it onto one person.[7]

No one relationship can handle the full weight of your needs, just as no building can be supported by a single, load-bearing column. We were designed for community, and that continues even into the world of dating and marriage.

The problem is that our overall attitude toward dating seems to be "my life, my business," leaving little—if any—room for other voices to speak into it. We live as though our dating life and our friendships are separate worlds. At a smaller level, I saw this with college couples who spent their time holed up in the student lounges or dorm rooms together, never spending time with other people. At a more extreme level, I knew someone who was a bridesmaid in her friend's wedding. Her first time meeting the groom—her friend's husband-to-be—was the day before the wedding. The marriage only lasted a few years. What we call "privacy" looks and smells an awful lot like isolation, just in a different form.

Sometimes, couples who let their friendships asphyxiate will feel lost after a breakup, or will avoid breaking up all together, not because the relationship is healthy, but because their social life outside of it isn't. When you make your partner your only friend, a break-up doesn't just mean the end of the relationship, but a return to social isolation.

We need to maintain other friendships as we date. Why? First, because love is blind. When you're in a romantic relationship with someone, you aren't able to see them through an objective lens. You will be inclined to think better of them, excuse and idealize what they do, and are more swayed by their words. When you date alone, behaviors such as grooming, gaslighting, or abuse are much harder to notice, especially when they come from someone you are attracted to. As one character from the show *BoJack Horseman* said, "when you look at someone through rose-colored glasses, all the red flags just look like flags."[8] The Apostle Paul warns, "The sins of some people are conspicuous, going before them to judgment, but the sins of others appear later" (1 Tim. 5:24). Some people are obviously trouble, but other flaws can be harder to notice right away.

"Where there is no guidance, a people falls, but in an abundance of counselors there is safety" (Prov. 11:14). Having trusted people around your relationship protects you, not only from unseen dangers, but from yourself. Sometimes, *you* are the one behaving unwisely. Sometimes, your expectations might be too harsh or too loose. Wise friends provide you with accountability and insight you couldn't find on your own.

In the Body of Christ, friends are a family God can use to speak through and grow us more into his image. Getting into a dating relationship, even entering into marriage, doesn't change this dynamic, nor should it give us a reason to step away. Quite the opposite: it should cause us to run toward it, to lean on our family in Christ. Listen to what the people you trust have to say. If we have done the work of letting our friends truly know us, and us truly trusting them, they will be one of our most valuable assets in dating and marriage.

OPPOSITE GENDER FRIENDSHIPS

Having friendships of the opposite gender can be a sensitive topic for some. The church has done a great job at encouraging physical boundaries, but it has struggled to communicate emotional boundaries. Avoiding sexual interaction or inappropriate physical contact is important, but so is maintaining healthy emotional boundaries. Given how little they are addressed, they might be a bigger deal than we think.

In my own life, I faced difficulties due to a lack of emotional boundaries. I had several female friends with whom I spent all my time. We would go on walks, see movies, eat out, and talk about everything. We would share our past regrets and personal struggles. I didn't hold much of myself back in those conversations. If you were to ask me if I liked them romantically, I would have said no, we were just friends.

And then, they would start dating other guys, and I'd instantly feel jealous. I put all these years of work into our friendship, only for some other guy to take it from me! With such a strong reaction, I had to realize that I had developed feelings for these women. Feelings snuck in without me realizing it. While we never said we were dating, we had been in an emotional relationship.

Between men and women, God built a desire for intimacy that naturally intensifies over time. The more time you spend together, especially one-on-one, and the deeper the conversations you have, the closer you will want to get with each other. This isn't bad—it's what leads to dating and marriage—but it's something we need to be cautious of. Some men and women may insist that very close friendships can exist without either falling for the other romantically. But, in my experience, it never stays that way. Nancy Wilson, writing to single women, issues a similar warning for friendships with men:

> Cultivate friendships in groups. Once you start pairing off, you are in danger of becoming too attached . . . don't grow fond in an unprotected setting. I have no idea how many times I have talked with women who were crushed when they found out that their "close friend" became engaged to someone else.[9]

A lack of boundaries leads to surprises, and not the good kinds. People want to go down the love tunnel, not a love detour. Because of the natural leaning for two separate genders to become one flesh, we must apply a degree of caution and care with our opposite-gender friends that we wouldn't need to with friends of the same gender.

Make no mistake, there is nothing wrong with having friends of the opposite gender. But there is a level of caution we must apply here. As a guy, certain things I do and say around women won't translate the same. If I take a guy out for dinner and talk about life with him, he will see that as intentional friendship. If I do the same for a woman, she will likely (and justifiably) see it as intentional romance. It doesn't have to look like "no girls allowed," it just means you have to be careful where you allow the girls to go emotionally.

Nancy Wilson makes an excellent recommendation: cultivate opposite-gender friendships in groups. If you desire to be married someday, marriage will change your friendships with the opposite gender. There's a reason why married men don't have close female friends, and why married women don't have close male friends: it heightens their risk for emotional infidelity, where extremely personal and private things are confided and someone you aren't married to begins to fill an emotional void that your spouse should occupy instead.

How do you know if your friendship has crossed over into unhealthy territory? A useful rule of thumb is the following question: if one of you were to marry someone else, would your friendship be appropriate?

THE NECESSITY OF FRIENDSHIPS

Our movies and television shows like to portray self-reliant heroes who save the world alone, but this couldn't be further from the life scripture encourages us to live. God didn't make us to be a lone wolf or a one-woman army, he fashioned us to flourish alongside other believers. So many biblical figures—including Jesus and Paul—didn't operate alone. They had friends: Jesus had his disciples, and Paul traveled with companions such as Silas and Timothy.

No one knows your need for people more than God. When we surround ourselves with friends who reflect Christ and bring out the best in us, we are setting ourselves on a path toward success. When we find friends, we aren't just finding people to have a good time with, but accountability partners, counselors, and comforters. Trust in God and follow where he leads you.

Here's an important truth you need to hear: if you don't have any close friends, then finding a boyfriend or a girlfriend will only add a plus one to your isolation—it will not free you. Without community outside of dating or marriage, our lives risk becoming consumed by the other person. In our desire for belonging and community, our partner can become our world. And that's far too much pressure for even the healthiest relationship.

This may sound harsh, but if you don't have close, godly friends whom you can trust with your faith life and your love life, then you shouldn't get into a dating relationship. If we lack depth in our non-romantic relationships, we lack sources of counsel and sustainment outside of our dating lives. When you encounter conflict or difficulties in your future relationships or marriage, what gets you through them won't be your affection for one other, but the skills you've both built as friends and the support of your other enduring friendships. You do not rise to the level of your romantic ambitions, you fall to the level of your friendships.[10]

Reflection Questions:

• What matters the most to you in a friend? What traits are the hardest to find in friendships?

• Do you tend to be more independent or dependent in your relationships? What would need to change for your friendships to become more interdependent?

• Would you trust the friends you currently have to speak into your dating life? Why or why not?

11

SEDUCTIVE FANTASIES

There's a brief conversation I had that challenged how I thought about romance.

I was in high school at the time. My dad and I were in the car together, and I was ecstatic. There was a girl from my youth group who I thought was attractive, and I had just received a text from her saying she felt the same way. Love at first notification. I was getting my dad caught up on the story when he interjected with a question.

"Could you imagine a future without this girl?"

I balked. Surely this had to be a test to see if I could envision this playing out long-term.

"No," I said confidently.

"Then that's a sign you're not ready to date yet," he said.

I was floored. I thought I had passed his test. Whatever could he mean by me not being ready? Wasn't it good to picture a future with the person you have a crush on?

Years later, I have come to appreciate my father's wisdom. He wasn't trying to dictate who I should or shouldn't date; he was calling attention to the fantasy I was weaving together. Despite barely knowing this girl, I was excited to the point where I couldn't envision a future without her.

When you become attracted to someone else, excitement about them is not only normal, but necessary. And yet, in our infatuation, we often overlook what it can do to our minds. Sometimes, the expectations we have arrive before a person does, and we try stretching the person to cover all of them. Whether it's in people or our pre-existing expectations, fantasies inform what we look for in love.

Infatuation and romantic desire are natural parts of life, but they can quickly spiral out of control, especially when left unchecked. Additionally, fantasies are difficult to diagnose. For one, they are often subconscious: we tend to fixate on the fantasy itself rather than the thought process that created it. However, when it comes to our relationship with Christ, our fantasies are important. Though we may not readily admit it, we can express self-control with our bodies but refuse to do the same with our minds. We can say "no" to sexual temptations while saying "yes" to far more extreme acts within the theater of our imagination. Regardless of how self-controlled we may try to live, our mental anarchism will often replicate itself in our external lives as well.

It's easy to dismiss fantasies as harmless. What's the harm in a little imagination? It may seem prudish to nitpick one's thoughts: surely thinking about sleeping with someone isn't as bad as actually having sex. But when it comes to sin, Jesus draws the line at our thoughts, not our actions. He warns, "You have heard that it was said, 'You shall not commit adultery.' But I say to you that everyone who looks at a woman with lustful intent has already committed adultery with her in his heart" (Matt. 5:27-28).

Our thoughts are formative: living like Jesus includes thinking like Jesus. It isn't just about the subject of our fantasies, it's also about the ideas and expectations they enforce. One of the best ways to understand how this plays out is by looking at the media in our culture.

MEDIA VS. REALITY

To say that media is significant is likely one of the biggest understatements you can make: according to one research firm, the average American adult consumes about twelve and a half hours of media every day, a number expected to grow to over thirteen and a half hours by 2026.[1] That may sound absurd, but media is far more than just movies and shows: it's the music you stream, the podcasts you listen to, the news you read, the social media you scroll through, and more.

Because of how ubiquitous media is, the way it influences us can be hard to notice. In fact, you might say to yourself, "What's the big deal? I'll watch and listen to whatever I want. Besides, it's not like it's affecting me at all." Music is music, movies are movies, and commercials are commercials . . . right? The truth is that we underestimate how much thought goes into crafting the media we consume, and how much that thought can actually influence us.

When we listen to a catchy song or watch an exciting movie, we usually don't think about the people who worked behind the scenes to make them as appealing and as exciting as possible. When we see celebrities on social media, we see the wealth and the happiness they appear to have and desire that for ourselves. But what we see online rarely reflects reality. Talk show host Conan O'Brien, who interacted with countless celebrities and influential people over the course of his career, voiced concerns about this disconnect.

> We have a culture that's constantly looking at our phones, at people that we think are so incredibly happy and have everything, and I will tell you for a fact the disparity—the difference between what they're projecting and how they are—is monumental.[2]

Media is a Latin word meaning "middle". It isn't a destination, it's a bridge—a medium. Media directs our imagination toward something. Everything, from the words we read to the images we see, is chosen to shape our thoughts or emotions in a certain direction. These narratives aren't necessarily good or bad, but they can affect our imagination in good or bad ways.

You don't have to look hard to guess what media says about love: I'm sure a few examples have already crossed your mind. Content like cheesy Hallmark movies can cause us to roll our eyes—it's easy to see stories like that are not realistic. But while anyone can poke fun at (or secretly enjoy) the absurdity of a Hallmark movie, there are other cues we often miss:

- Magazines featuring the latest celebrity couple
- Commercials highlighting couples or families with phrases like "protect the ones you treasure most"
- Ads for dating apps and "hot singles in your area"
- Pinterest boards for weddings and date night ideas
- Music from artists lamenting over a breakup or lusting over a sexual prospect
- Movies where a character finds love (or rekindles it) as part of their happy ending

- Online videos or articles promising skills, secrets, or products to make you romantically irresistible
- Romance novels depicting idealized (and often erotic) portrayals of love
- Reality shows where the "winners" get married
- Photos of couples or families you know where everyone looks beautiful and happy
- A friend's relationship update on social media

On their own, these appear inconsequential. However, when these cues are considered altogether or experienced frequently, they paint a strong picture which can inform our expectations for love and inflame our desire to experience it.

Media often depicts love based on what's ideal instead of what's real. We think we're getting more in touch with reality, when in actuality we're buying into a fiction. It convinces us our fantasies are feasible. Most of the time, we overlook how fine-tuned media can be to our fantasies.

Take Flynn Rider from the Disney movie *Tangled*. He's attractive, charming, and incredibly skilled. He's the classic bad boy who secretly has a softer side. But Flynn isn't real: he's manufactured. As the film's directors worked on the movie, they held "hot man meetings" with dozens of women to craft a man designed to be irresistible.[3] Flynn is made to be the ideal man. He *seems* real (an actual man voiced him, after all), but he's still a fantasy, a product.

Media shapes our fantasies into tangible desires. We may know what we're watching is orchestrated and not real, but we have still *seen* it. Our eyes register the images as visual "evidence" that the fantasy exists, even if it's only an illusion.

My friend, Megan, experienced this firsthand while looking for a husband. She admitted that the Disney movies she watched as a kid influenced her expectations for marriage. "My parents painted that picture to me. Even though they did not show that picture, that's what they spoke. They spoke that picture, but they never acted out that picture."

She eventually found a husband, but their marriage quickly turned toxic. "What I had in my head about marriage was not what I actually had in my marriage." He clung to her, isolating them from everyone else in their life. She wanted them to practice their faith together, but he wasn't interested. She explained:

> Growing up on Disney, you expect happiness . . .
> worshipping together and doing devotions and growing
> together in Christ . . . I did not have any of that. It was a
> battle to pick a church, it was a battle to tithe, it was a
> battle to even read a Bible passage together. It was far from
> the ideals that I had.[4]

It's not like we will want exactly what we see on the screen. In Megan's case, the Disney movies she saw at a young age didn't mean she was looking for a literal prince wearing armor and riding on a white horse. But the devil of our expectations is in the details—the way the couples' physical attractiveness, the effortless banter and dialogue— which can give a tangible form to our yearnings. We're aware that looking for a Princess or a Prince Charming isn't realistic, but we inundate ourselves with content where they're right there, flesh and bone. Abstract ideas given form.

THE MYTH OF "THE ONE"

When we believe a fantasy for long enough, its roots grow deep. The fantasy becomes a myth: a lie close enough to the truth that many of us believe it. One such myth that holds sway over many struggling romantics is that of "The One".

The One is the ideal romantic match. This myth is known by many names: your soulmate, your true love, Mr. or Ms. Right, your twin flame, your heart's desire, the man or woman of your dreams, and so on. Countless songs, films, and books refer to this idea that the perfect match is out there somewhere waiting for you.

This belief is incredibly popular in our culture. In a recent poll, 60% of Americans said they believe in soulmates.[5] You have likely heard it in conversation before: the single girl dreaming with her friends about what her "one" might be like. The broken-hearted man talking to his friends about his ex: "I thought she was 'the one'." A single woman's parents mentioning an eligible man: "He might be 'the one' for you!" For most people, The One isn't a myth. It's reality, an inevitability.

Using "The One" as shorthand for "The One I Will Eventually Marry"—as in "future spouse"—is fine. However, we rarely stop there. We imagine how this "One" will look, how they will make us feel, and the ways they will show us their love. In doing so, "The One" progresses from a nice thought into a detailed fantasy. We start to believe that "The One" is not just a future spouse but a source of ultimate fulfillment.

One of the biggest problems with this is that no person on earth can fulfill us in this way. We aren't chasing a physical person but an elusive fiction. This has led to immeasurable heartbreak and dissatisfaction. Even the poet who came up with the term "soulmate" had a miserable marriage.[6] This pain is because we're looking for perfection, which we can never find in a human being. This typically leads to shifting the goalposts—continuously redefining who "The One" actually is.

"I want someone hot."

"Okay, she's hot but not smart. She's got to be smart."

"Alright, she might have a college degree, but she doesn't *sound* smart."

"Okay, now she sounds *too* smart."

The priority becomes getting everything we want and refusing to compromise. After all, "The One" will check all the boxes, right? One guy I knew dated a woman who seemed amazing. Then, one day, the woman ended the relationship. Her reason? She wanted to live near the beach and sensed he wouldn't want to move there. I heard another story about a guy who hesitated to marry an incredible, godly woman because she had, according to him, "flabby arms".

From the outside, it's easy to spot the ridiculousness. None of us are perfect, and there will always be flaws to find. But in the eyes of a perfectionist whose imagination is fueled by fantasies of the ideal soulmate, every flaw is a sign that The One is still out there.

Plus, in our search for the perfect match, there's a hidden hypocrisy. We want someone to be The One for us, but we seldom consider being The One for someone else. It's a one-way street: we want a perfect person, yet assume we won't have any flaws that will turn them away. We never stop to think, "Would I pass the test I'm giving everyone I date?" We're so busy asking "what if someone better comes along?" That we never stop to ask ourselves, "how can I be someone better for them?"

By looking for The One, we are pursuing the ghost of perfection and find only pain, heartbreak, and unmet expectations. The people we pursue become nothing more than placeholders until someone better comes along. We constantly shift the goalposts for love interests without considering how far we're asking them to run. And the worst part is that this fantasy affects our expectations not only for love, but for God.

THE REAL SOULMATE

If we were to list all the qualities of an ideal partner—putting aside all the preferences of eye color, height, build, and desire to live near the beach—we might say we want someone who:

- Effortlessly and deeply understands you
- Delights in being with you
- Says the right things at the right times
- Seeks ways to intimately express love to you
- Fulfills your needs selflessly and unexpectedly
- Never leaves your side, no matter the circumstance
- Looks past your flaws and is quick to forgive
- Loves others without getting distracted from loving you
- Is always present in conversation, empathetically listening as long as you need

When combined, this list of extraordinary traits creates an expectation that no human being can ever fully measure up to. But, if you reread the list, you'll find that God easily fulfills each and every criteria. These expectations aren't human-sized, they are God-sized.

Only in Christ alone can we find what our hearts yearn for. This is demonstrated in an encounter Jesus has with a woman at a well. She has been through five husbands and is currently living with a man she isn't married to. She has been looking for love and hasn't found it in any of the men she's been with. Instead of shaming or shunning her, Jesus offers her something incredible: a peek inside her soul and the solution for her struggles.

> Jesus said to her, "Everyone who drinks of this water will be thirsty again, but whoever drinks of the water that I will give him will never be thirsty again. The water that I will give him will become in him a spring of water welling up to eternal life."

(John 4:13-14)

The woman had a desire that no man could satisfy. She was seeking out short-term solutions to an eternal problem. Like her, we seek a human substitute for the goodness of God, but there is no substitute, not even close.

Saltwater and freshwater both fill you with water, but drinking saltwater leads to dehydration. If we try to drink saltwater, we will always be thirsty. Only in freshwater will our thirst be truly quenched. If we are searching for another human being to fill our deep thirst for intimacy, we will never be fully satisfied. Only Christ is sufficient. His love is deep and wide enough to fill our God-sized expectations. You will have all your inner longings satisfied, all your thirst quenched. The love he brings into our lives will never fail us:

it will increase, it will "become . . . a spring of water welling up to eternal life." What Christ offers sounds too good to be true, but in him it actually *is* true.

As mythical as we can make it, The One is a product of false expectations fueled by our own heart. Proverbs urges us to "guard your heart, for everything you do flows from it" (Prov. 4:23 NIV). Our heart isn't completely out of our control. The solution doesn't necessarily lie in cutting media completely out of our lives, but it does mean we need to watch how we engage with it.

We are made as reflections of a creative and imaginative God. The problem is not our mind, it's what we're feeding it. We must "take every thought captive to obey Christ" (2 Cor. 10:5). It isn't wrong to watch a Disney film, but we need to watch how it affects our thoughts. Paul says, "whatever is true, whatever is honorable, whatever is just, whatever is pure, whatever is lovely, whatever is commendable, if there is any excellence, if there is anything worthy of praise, think about these things" (Phil. 4:8).

When we fantasize about a person who can save us, it distracts us from the one who already has. Being captivated by beauty is good unless it captivates us away from the truth. By buying into a fantasy instead of reality, we limit our pleasure and fulfillment of our desires to The One instead of The One True God.

Reflection Questions:

• What media do you spend most of your time with? What narratives or "cues" about love have you noticed in the media you engage with? What do they tell you about love?

• Is there a movie or show you've watched that has a character you find attractive? Which traits of theirs are realistic? Which traits are unrealistic?

• Look at the list of traits on pg. 141. Which of these do you desire the most in a future spouse? Which of these feel the most unattainable to you?

• Only in Jesus can your thirst for relational intimacy be fully quenched. What emotions does this statement bring up for you? What hesitations do you have with it?

12

WORSHIPPING WITH OUR BODIES

My grandma has a hard time understanding smartphones. When she first got an iPhone, she would completely power it off when she wasn't using it, completely defeating the purpose of having a phone to begin with. Despite how capable the machine in her hands was, she would only use it to call people or send an occasional text message. Was she doing this because she hated using technology? Certainly not. There were just too many features for her to learn. For me—someone who grew up with smartphones—it was mind-blowing. While my grandma was using her iPhone in ways it was designed, she didn't grasp that it was made for so much more.

As Christians, we often see worship in the same way. We think it's praising God through song, without realizing it's about so much more. When I was younger, that's all I thought worship was: singing and dancing. I associated worship with musical performance or, more accurately, musical *reaction*. If I didn't sing or dance as enthusiastically as those around me, then worship must not be for me.

But, much like my grandma and her iPhone, this understanding of worship only scratches the surface. Praising

God through music is certainly *one* way to worship, but it is far from the *only* way. Worship isn't an activity so much as it is a response, a way of life. As David Foster Wallace points out, Christians aren't the only ones who worship, either.

> There is no such thing as not worshipping. Everybody worships. The only choice we get is what to worship . . . pretty much anything else you worship will eat you alive. If you worship money and things, if they are where you tap real meaning in life, then you will never have enough, never feel you have enough. It's the truth. Worship your body and beauty and sexual allure and you will always feel ugly. And when time and age start showing, you will die a million deaths before they finally grieve you . . . Worship power, you will end up feeling weak and afraid, and you will need ever more power over others to numb you to your own fear. Worship your intellect, being seen as smart, you will end up feeling stupid, a fraud, always on the verge of being found out . . . They're the kind of worship you just gradually slip into, day after day, getting more and more selective about what you see and how you measure value without ever being fully aware that that's what you're doing.[1]

While Wallace wasn't a Christian, his words are spot-on. Anything can be an object of worship: our career, our marital status, and even ministry work. The problem is, as Wallace mentioned, we can slip into worshipping something else if we're not careful. We can think we're seeking God when we're actually replacing him with an idol. As God declares, "I am the Lord . . . my glory I give to no other, nor my praise to carved idols" (Is. 42:8). Seeking God's glory and worshipping him is a continuous and conscious choice.

The question isn't *if* you worship, it's *what* you worship. When we value something to the extent that we give our time and energy to it, define ourselves by it, and prioritize it above all else, we are worshipping it. When we love something, we commit our time, our money, and our energy to ensure it flourishes. Look at where you spend most of your time each day, what you watch the most on social media, or what you constantly think about and look forward to. Whatever you give the most to is what you love, and what you love, you worship.

PHYSICAL WORSHIP

Odds are, when given the chance to describe sex, few of us would consider it a form of worship. And yet, we idolize it to where our culture is often labeled as "hypersexualized." Casual sex has gone from a taboo subject to an accepted practice. Instead of condemning extramarital sex, we now condemn any boundaries placed upon it. "If I want to sleep with someone, who are you to tell me otherwise?" Caution has given way to expectation, and expectation has given way to entitlement. Sexual fulfillment is now treated like a human right.

The fallout of this entitlement affects everyone. One younger girl was taken aback at how many guys were attempting to pressure her into sex over social media. She blocked a guy, so he made another account to continue pressuring her. It got so bad she thought about caving in just to make their demands go away. In this context, sex has become a means of gratifying ourselves at the expense of others. The only thing that matters is getting what we want. It's sickening.

That story was an extreme example; sexual entitlement is often far more subtle. It's woven into the fabric of our cultural philosophy that says, "I have sexual needs that must be fulfilled. Therefore, any limitations on them are oppressive and unhealthy." Restraint is seen as impossible, if not downright harmful. In fact, many believe that if you are not sexually fulfilled, you cannot have a meaningful life. In his book, one secular therapist bluntly encouraged singles to "go out and f*ck someone".[2] Ironically, culture claims that the Bible treats sex with disdain, when it is actually the culture itself doing this.

This doesn't just pertain to sexual intercourse. In fact, fewer people are having sex. But, as Mark Regnerus argues, this simply reflects the fact that "more men and women are delaying marriage—hence limiting their access to a stable partner—and more are finding satiation in the dopamine hits that come from social media consumption or from masturbation."[3] Our worship of sex is far more than intercourse, it's evident in pornography, masturbation, sexually provocative media . . . anything and everything done in the name of achieving sexual satisfaction.

This permissiveness has trickled into churches as well. One study of American Christians found that only about a third thought sex between unmarried adults was "never okay," regardless if it happened inside a committed relationship or not.[4] Instead of adjusting the way we live to accommodate the Word of God, we adjust the Word of God to accommodate the way we live. Rather than condemn unbiblical sexual practices amongst Christians, we treat sex more like politics at family meals: we understand that it's out there and impacts our lives, but it's best to avoid bringing it up.

This attitude toward sex is rooted in the idea that what we believe spiritually has no bearing on what we do physically—that faith is a matter of the heart and mind, not the body. The Bible, however, makes no such distinction. In fact, Paul openly challenges this assumption, asking, "do you not know that your body is a temple of the Holy Spirit within you, whom you have from God? You are not your own, for you were bought with a price. So glorify God in your body" (1 Cor. 6:19-20). Because of our relationship with Jesus, the Holy Spirit resides in our bodies. Therefore, our bodies are holy and set apart for God, and we must worship God with them accordingly.

If you are a Christian, your body is a temple: what you do with it reflects how you treat God. It can be strange to think of worship in both a spiritual and physical sense, but the Bible gives a robust picture of this. "I appeal to you therefore . . . to present your bodies as a living sacrifice, holy and acceptable to God, which is your spiritual worship" (Rom. 12:1). Paul isn't saying our *beliefs* are a holy and acceptable sacrifice, he is explicitly referring to our *bodies*. When we sacrifice something, we freely give it up. In order for us to live sacrificially, we must give up any bodily desires that get in the way of God's desires. In other words, worshipping God affects the relationship we have with our bodies, and a right relationship with our bodies is a way we worship God.

Worship isn't limited to Sunday services or Bible studies. It encompasses every part of our lives, including the bedroom.

THE MYTH OF CASUAL SEX

Nothing brings two humans together more completely and intimately than sex. Scientific research shows that during sex, hormones such as vasopressin and oxytocin are released. These hormones promote bonding and attachment, functioning a lot like emotional super glue.[5] Within marriage, sex amplifies the couple's connection to each other—it was designed by God to exclusively exist within commitment. Outside of marriage, however, it can cause people to remain in bad relationships longer and makes breakups emotionally and biologically devastating. Kat Harris sums it up: "There really is, neurologically, no such thing as casual sex."[6]

God created sex as a bond, specifically to unite a husband and wife so they become one flesh (Gen. 2:24). Does this mean they are now the same person? Sort of. Differences obviously remain within marriage. The husband may enjoy steak, the wife may not. The wife may enjoy romantic comedies, the husband may not. While superficial aspects of the married couple may remain different, sex brings its participants together not only physically, but spiritually.

This aspect of marriage—the joining together of male and female, of two lives into one—has a deeper beauty and purpose. Paul explains, "This mystery is profound, and I am saying that it refers to Christ and the church" (Eph. 5:32). The togetherness that sex brings between spouses is a glimpse into our future togetherness with Christ. It's a foretaste, a preview of a much greater intimacy. To violate the design of marriage is to violate what it says about God.

When we decide to pursue sex on our terms, when we focus on obtaining glory for ourselves instead of giving it to God, then we are worshipping our own desires. Scripture teaches that sex was designed to be exclusively between one man and one woman within the covenant of marriage.

When we see sex as a symbol of Christ's relationship with the church, other questions about sexual practice become clear. Why does it have to be in the covenant of marriage? Because God made a covenant with us, first through Abraham and later through Jesus. Why does it have to be between two people instead of three or more? Because our relationship with God is exclusive, without anything else competing for our worship. Why does it require a male and female instead of a male and a male or a female and a female? Because Jesus wasn't sent to unite with himself, and we weren't saved so we could unite with ourselves: Jesus died and resurrected so *we* could be united with *him*, so heaven could be united with earth. When you mess with marriage, you mess with what it represents. There is nothing casual about sex (for specific ways we compromise the design of sex, see Appendix II).

WE'RE ALL GUILTY

When I was in high school, I received my first ever paycheck. It was a few hundred dollars, which was the most amount of money I'd ever had at that point. The possibilities of what I could spend it on were intoxicating. I ended up going on a shopping spree and bought over three hundred dollars worth of Nerf guns. Brimming with excitement, I brought all the packages into my bedroom and began opening them. It felt like a self-imposed Christmas. I was truly content and happy . . .

. . . for about five minutes. Then, as I considered the mound of toys I had purchased, a feeling of emptiness washed over me. I realized I didn't have anyone I could play with. Sure, I could shoot at some targets, but I wouldn't enjoy my Nerf guns to the fullest extent. There I sat, alone, with a mixture of plastic and disappointment. I had wasted my time and money on something that hadn't brought the satisfaction I was looking for.

When we worship something finite and imperfect, such as sex, it will never completely satisfy us. Like my shopping spree, we can acquire all the sex we want and have all our fantasies satiated, but it won't be enough. When we act outside of God's design, we hurt ourselves. Even the therapist I quoted earlier admits that rampant sex "doesn't lead to fulfillment . . . it leads to feelings of loneliness and to cravings for something deeper. It's not sustainable."[7]

There's a famous saying: "love the sinner, hate the sin." It's accurate, yet the western church has an unfortunate history in terms of how it has dealt with sexual brokenness. Many men and women who have fallen short of God's sexual ethic have been harmed, ostracized, and villainized. More recently, some churches have pivoted. Those who were ostracized have now been affirmed, validated, and excused. When it comes to the sinner and the sin, we have a history of either hating both or loving both.

Neither of these extremes were modeled by Jesus. On one hand, he forgave and showed mercy to sinners. When a woman caught in adultery was brought before him, Jesus doesn't condemn her, but told her "Go, and from now on sin no more" (John 8:3-11). Jesus' ministry embodied love and forgiveness, yet he also drew lines with sexuality that many westerners would find too restrictive, such as when he said, "everyone who looks at a woman with lustful intent has already committed adultery with her in his heart" (Matt. 5:28). Jesus wasn't afraid to call sin "sin," but he was also quick to extend forgiveness. He neither compromised on truth nor on love.

That's the point of the Gospel. We have *all* fallen short of God's law. We have looked at what we shouldn't have. We have done things and had things done to us that we still feel the weight of. Chances are, if you're reading this, you have fallen short sexually in one way or another. I remember talking to a friend years ago who had messed up sexually. She was devastated and utterly filled with shame. As she told me what had happened, she bemoaned, "I thought I was a good Christian girl."

You might feel the same way. If you do, I want you to understand there is no such thing as a "good Christian": to be a Christian is to be a work in progress. We think Jesus only wants the perfect, religious people, but he himself said he came for the sick and the imperfect (Mark 2:17). Jesus loves you: it's why he is pursuing you in the first place! There is nothing you've done that he can't wipe away. You aren't too tainted or too broken to be accepted by him.

God's law doesn't exist to push sinners away, but to expose the depth of sin in each and every one of us—and to point us to a more fulfilling way to live. We need to grasp the gravity of our sin while recognizing the power Jesus has to save us from it. If we don't understand how much we've fallen short, we won't appreciate how much Jesus sacrificed so we could be with him. When we understand that and respond with reverence and adoration for the new life we have in him, that's worship.

A SINGLE'S GUIDE TO SEX

No one loves sex more than God. That sentence may cause you to question everything you've read so far and think, "Goodness, Daniel really went off the rails." But it's true! Not the part about me, I hope, but the part about God and sex. God created sex and marriage: they were his idea. As the designer of sex, God should have the final say on its expression. He knows how sex is best enjoyed. Why *wouldn't* we follow his instructions on how to best experience it?

As G.K. Chesterton observed, "the more I considered Christianity, the more I found that, while it had established a rule and order, the chief aim of that order was to give room for good things to run wild."[8] The restrictions God places in our lives are so we can thrive and flourish. When we violate the design of sex, we not only sin against God, but we are unable to enjoy sex to its fullest extent. The picture God has for sex, within marriage, is something that is thrilling, delightful, and life-giving.

How can we worship God without being ensnared by sexual sin? Scripture is clear: "Flee from sexual immorality.

Every other sin a person commits is outside the body, but the sexually immoral person sins against his own body" (1 Cor. 6:18). Your body is a temple. The question is, what is that temple devoted to? Who or what is allowed in the temple? For us singles, sexual immorality is participation in any kind of erotic activity. We aren't married, so what may be permissible for married couples is not permissible for us. When we prioritize our bodily desires above God, we become hostile to him and cannot please him (Rom. 8:6-8).

In our hypersexualized culture, it's a hard line to hold. Many Christians today assume that, if God's will contradicts how we feel, then God must be wrong. If the reality of scripture doesn't line up with the reality we're experiencing, we resort to fight or flight: either we flee from the text convicting us or we attack it, altering its context or insisting it's invalid. Either way, we try everything within our power to eliminate our tension with the text.

But God is eternal. His wisdom is consistently true across time and history. If God says a heterosexual, monogamous marriage is the intended environment for sex, then that doesn't just apply to people in biblical times, but for all of us today.

James urges us to "submit yourselves therefore to God. Resist the devil, and he will flee from you" (4:7). Submitting to God means listening and carrying out his words. It means acknowledging his authority over your life. If we feel tension between following God or following our desires, it isn't a sign that we've misinterpreted scripture or that the Bible is irrelevant, it's an indicator that we are starting to place our desires above God's. It's us debating who we really want to worship.

If worship is spiritual *and* physical, your relationship with your body is important. This is something that must be done prayerfully. Paul says "husbands should love their wives as their own bodies. He who loves his wife loves himself. For no one ever hated his own flesh, but nourishes and cherishes it, just as Christ does the church" (Eph. 5:28-29). If a husband does not treat his own body in a healthy, godly manner, then he will have difficulty treating his wife's body in the same way. How do you treat your own body? If you gratify its every whim, you will treat sex in your marriage the same way. The relationship you have with your body will impact the relationship you'll have with your future spouse's body.

Paul ends one of his letters by saying, "may the God of peace himself sanctify you completely, and may your whole spirit and soul and body be kept blameless at the coming of our Lord Jesus Christ. He who calls you is faithful; *he will surely do it*" (1 Thess. 5:23-24, emphasis mine). None of us can live blameless lives on our own. It is a work of the Holy Spirit, who resides within the temples of our bodies. The question is whether or not we will allow the Spirit to continue his sanctifying work within us.

There is nothing that cannot be redeemed by God. He is able to take your life, warts and all, and fashion it into a beautiful monument of his love. Nothing about you surprises God. Nothing. Your past trauma does not compromise his plan for your life. Your mistakes and current struggles don't repulse him. When he says he wants a relationship with you, he knows exactly what he's getting into. He knows what he's doing, and he does it because he loves you. We must stop trying to find love in sex and start finding it by worshipping the God who loves us as we already are.

Reflection Questions:

• What relationship do you have with your body? Do you indulge it too much? Do you neglect it? How could you treat it more like a temple?

• What part of God's design for sex do you struggle with the most? Why is that part hard for you?

• How have you fallen short of God's sexual standard? Is there sin that you have a hard time accepting that God has forgiven? Spend time in prayer. Confess your sin to God and ask him to forgive you and to remind you of his love.

13

EMOTIONAL HORNINESS

I'll never forget when I was stuck in an airport for sixteen hours.

I arrived early in the morning, got through security, and waited for my flight to arrive. I was going to see my family for Christmas. Then, my phone buzzed. My flight was delayed by an hour. No worries, I could wait for a bit longer for my layover flight. Then, it buzzed again: I would have to switch flights and wait three hours or so. Not the end of the world. Then, five minutes later, this flight, too, was cancelled. An attendant told me the next available flight wasn't until eleven that night.

That's when I knew I was in for an incredibly long day.

Leaving the airport and coming back wasn't an option: I had been dropped off and didn't want to sentence some poor soul to drive me back late at night. It was the holiday season, so I couldn't exchange my ticket for a different one. Besides, there was no guarantee I could find an earlier flight at another airport. There was nothing for me to do but wait.

So, wait I did.

As it turns out, you can learn some interesting things when you spend all day at the airport. For one, if you set the bar low enough, you can occupy yourself with anything. The airport was incredibly tiny, with only three restaurants. I tried them all. I sat in all the different areas you could sit. I journaled. I prayed for time to speed up. I read an entire book. Later in the evening, to treat myself, I browsed the souvenir shop.

The hours slogged by. The sun began to sink beneath the horizon. The amount of people in the airport became fewer and fewer. Stores began to shut down, including my beloved souvenir shop. My parents, who had been calling to check in and make sure I wasn't going insane, tucked in for the night. It was just me now, alone with my thoughts. There was no one else to talk to. Slowly, eleven o'clock drifted closer.

Then, my phone buzzed. Another delay. My plane was now arriving at midnight. I stared at the nondescript ceiling, despair seeping into my exhausted brain. *How much longer must I wait?!* Each second felt like an eternity. I was running out of ways to distract myself. I began to feel a kinship with Tom Hanks's character in *The Terminal*. Is purgatory real? Did I die, and now I'm stuck here forever?

As midnight approached, my phone buzzed again. The flight had been pushed back to one in the morning. My spirits sank to their lowest point all day. I'd been trapped in the airport for fourteen hours at this point and my feelings of despair were growing. It was late at night, so I couldn't call anyone. *What if this flight gets cancelled?* I tried fighting the thought, but it persisted. Worst-case scenarios began playing out in my mind. *When would I be able to sleep again?* I thought of all the families who were already celebrating the holidays together and sleeping in nice, warm beds. And I was there at the airport, alone and helpless. There was nothing I could do: I was completely at the mercy of forces well beyond my control.

There is a distinct existential pain in singleness that is difficult to explain to those who don't experience it. It's more than loneliness. It's a deep heartache, a painful craving for a depth of intimacy that few things seem able to distract from coupled with the dread that you will never experience such a thing.[1]

This emotional agony is frustratingly unpredictable, triggered almost at random. It could be an attractive stranger, a friend's wedding, an announcement on social media, a romantic movie scene, or a cute couple passing by. At times it can be stirred by nothing at all, emerging in quiet moments alone. You don't necessarily desire a specific person, you just *desire*. A guy I knew referred to this longing as "emotional horniness".

For all the blessings and advantages singleness brings, this deep yearning is a burden that never fully goes away. It isn't always conscious, but when it hits, it hits deep. Many struggling romantics feel it, but few bring it up. Some feel too ashamed to discuss this emotional ache because they want to avoid sounding repetitive, even when around fellow singles. For all the resources on singleness out there, this is one area many rarely address.

When we experience this "emotional horniness", it can feel a lot like being trapped in an airport, waiting for something you fear will never arrive. The marriage—the person—you're waiting for hasn't shown up, only unexpected delays. You're in your darkest hour, looking at the clock, wondering if anyone knows you're still there. Most of your friends—maybe all of them—are already at the destination you're trying to get to, but you're still waiting, feeling left behind, wondering if you'll ever get out.

There are three primary prescriptions people give for this profound emotional ache. One is repression: this feeling will prohibit you from being content in your singleness, so you must distract yourself with something productive or deny it exists altogether. Give it to the Lord and move on. Another is reductionism: this feeling must be the result of lust or some lesser desire. It's a stumbling block interfering with your ability to only desire God and nothing else; therefore, it's a sign your relationship with God needs correction. The final prescription is rehabilitation: if you want a spouse so bad, go find one already; and stop overthinking your feelings. Shut up and do something about it, otherwise, you'll only make it worse for yourself. In other words, the emotional ache is either a trivial distraction, a symptom of sin, or a result of immaturity.

There are indeed singles who tend to be unproductive, overthink their feelings, and struggle with lust. However, these problems arise from responses to the ache, not the ache itself. As it turns out, our "emotional horniness" isn't a byproduct of sin nor immaturity, but a result of how God wired us as human beings. It isn't just a natural desire, but one *deliberately given to us by God.*

THE PROBLEM IN PARADISE

We can actually find evidence of this desire for intimacy within the Bible's first few pages, in the book of Genesis. In the beginning, God makes everything under the sun (not to mention the sun itself). After God creates something, he calls it "good". He dots the sky with stars, sculpts the earth, populates it with creatures, and then crafts Adam and sets him to work in the garden. All of this is good. But then, God says, "It is *not* good that the man should be alone; I will make him a helper fit for him" (Gen. 2:18, emphasis mine).

This is a jarring contrast to earlier. Did God say this because Adam was struggling with lust? No, because sin had not yet entered the world. At this point, Adam was a perfect man. He wasn't immature or flawed. His productivity wasn't the problem, either, because he was naming the animals and doing exactly what God had made him to do (Gen. 2:19). Adam himself wasn't the issue. If he was, God would have replaced him or fixed him so he wouldn't feel this way. Nor was it an issue of Adam's relationship with God. They experienced perfect communion in the garden, uninhibited by sin. The loneliness God sees in Adam isn't a flaw on Adam's part nor is it a mistake on God's part.

So why did God say this was "not good"?

The answer is not because Adam botched God's design, but rather because he fulfilled it. When God decides to create Adam, he says, "Let *us* make man in our image, after *our* likeness" (Gen. 1:26, emphasis mine). By referring to himself as "us", God is referring to the Trinity, being both himself, Jesus, and the Holy Spirit: three distinct persons in one. God himself exists in community, and he designed Adam to flourish in the same way. Although Adam had what was likely the most intimate relationship with God anyone on this side of heaven (save for Jesus himself) has ever had, he still needed other people like him. By feeling this way, Adam was demonstrating he was an image-bearer of God.

God could have wired us to be completely satisfied in him, to not desire community at all. And yet, he gave us a yearning for human connection, for intimacy with one another—and marriage is the fullest and greatest expression of this desire. In short, to long for marriage—for deep connection—is a reflection of the way God made us.

THE PARADOX IN SINGLENESS

Your desires for marriage, for sex, for children, for intimacy . . . none of these are intrinsically evil. Far from it. God has woven within us a yearning to be known and loved by other humans in addition to being known and loved by God. We can't ignore our feelings—or at least we can't for long. Trying to "suck it up" and pretend our longing doesn't exist will only lead to misery. Instead, we need to accept that God has deliberately given us this desire. It's a reminder that you are created in his image.

And yet, this raises even more questions. What then should we do with this longing? Why doesn't God give us a spouse to satisfy this desire if he designed us to experience intimacy?

As struggling romantics, we face a unique dilemma: if we neglect our yearning for marriage, we ignore a God-given desire; but if we neglect our singleness, we ignore a God-given gift. Reconciling our singleness with our aching to leave it behind feels like an impossible balancing act, an inherent contradiction in terms.

To make matters more complicated, the world isn't going to stand still so we can take the time to figure this out. Your closest friend gets married and you realize there's one less single in your life. Your family asks if you're dating someone. Your friends try to set you up with another single they swear you'll actually like. You go to singles groups that feel more like speed-dating events. Your dating app tells you someone is 99% compatible with you, and then your date with them tells you they are 0% compatible with you. Little moments like these build pressure. Time is running out, and we feel our days being numbered, our window of opportunity closing.

When I went to a private Christian college, nothing could prepare me for the wave of matrimony that hit. It was like watching a romantic tsunami: single people went from the majority to the outlier in what felt like a nanosecond. To paint a picture of how ridiculous it was, I ran into an acquaintance from college one summer. I asked her what she did to fight the long summer days. She replied, "Well, I work on the weekdays, but on the weekends, I go to weddings."

"How come? Are you a wedding planner?" I asked.

"No," she said, "So many of my friends are getting married in the summer, that there's been a wedding every weekend."

With so many weddings, it's easy to feel like you're running behind. It's almost like marriage is a train that everyone is jumping onto, and you're terrified you may not make it before the train leaves the station. Combine that with getting older and not yet being married, and singleness goes from an endearing part of youth to an isolating time-bomb culminating in old age and death.

So, what can we do? Oftentimes, we compensate. We try even harder to seek out a spouse. Every time we see a new member of the opposite gender around our age, we try and sneak a glance at their left ring finger to see if they are "taken" or not. When we hear of a "singles mixer" at a nearby church or try a new dating app, we vacillate between speculative hope that we may finally find our future spouse and paranoia that our desperation will be too obvious.

None of this addresses the pain we feel: it only serves to keep us distracted. The only way to truly address this despair is to address the hurt beneath it. When I feel despair pulling my heart into the abyss, I need more than platitudes like "just lean on God" or "give it to Jesus and you'll be okay"—I need truth.

THE POWERFUL COMFORT OF GOD

There's a story in the Old Testament that gives us a framework for addressing moments of significant emotional pain. The prophet Elijah had just publicly displayed that God was more powerful than Ba'al, a pagan god the Israelites were worshipping.

But Elijah's victory doesn't last long. The Queen, herself a follower of Ba'al, threatens his life. Afraid, Elijah runs off into the wilderness. In contrast to earlier, he is dejected. He is alone and filled with despair, to the point where he pleads for God to take his life. He has obeyed God and done everything he can think of doing, and it still doesn't feel like enough.

Watch how God ministers to Elijah in this state. First, he sends an angel who provides Elijah with food, touching him and saying, "Arise and eat" (1 Kings 19:5). Elijah does so, and after letting him rest, the angel urges him to do the same a second time. Here, God starts by tending to Elijah's biological needs: he literally cooks for Elijah. He has Elijah rest. Sometimes, when we ache, that's all we need: a hearty meal, a walk outside, a good book, a warm hug, a long nap.

Strengthened by the food, Elijah moves into a cave. This time, the word of the Lord comes to him and asks what he is doing there. Elijah tells him, and the word of the Lord replies, "Go out and stand on the mount before the Lord" (v.11). This time, God is inviting Elijah to be with him. When a simple meal or a hike won't do, you might need community. Sharing our burdens with close friends or mentors can provide us with wisdom and reassurance. Sometimes, just being in the presence of others or doing something fun with them can comfort our hurting soul.

Finally, we see God's third approach to healing Elijah's emotional wounds. As Elijah stands on the mountain, he encounters a great wind, an earthquake, and a fire, but God isn't in any of them. Then, in the wake of these fearsome storms, God appears in a soft whisper. As he speaks, God not only gives Elijah directions on what to do next, but also gives him hope. "I will leave seven thousand in Israel, all the knees that have not bowed to Ba'al, and every mouth that has not kissed him" (v. 18). God reassures Elijah that he is not alone: others are resisting the pagan god.

God addresses Elijah's spiritual needs gently, not forcefully. He appears not as a fearsome storm, but as a gentle whisper. He gives Elijah spiritual reassurance, but only after Elijah has been physically and emotionally restored. Spiritual healing is necessary, and there are times when we need to deal with our emotional ache by hearing God's truth and love through reading scripture, listening to worship music, or praying (Appendix I is an example of a prayer for moments like these).

God doesn't chastise Elijah for having weak faith. He could have said, "Snap out of it, Elijah. I am the Lord. Read the scriptures and get back out there." After all, Elijah witnessed the incredible power of God one chapter before! Instead, God demonstrates a multidimensional approach to comforting and healing Elijah's inner pain.

In our culture, we have a tendency to overspiritualize our problems. We can say "I need to read my Bible more" or "maybe I just need to pray more than I've been doing"; and sometimes we're right, but not always. As C.S. Lewis describes, "Humans are amphibians—half spirit and half animal."[2] We are beings made in both spirit and body: sometimes we need to tend to our spiritual hurts and other times our physical ones. Trying to treat everything as a spiritual wound is like taking the same medication for every disease.

THE PRACTICE OF TRUSTING GOD

For a while, I believed that my desire for marriage and being content in my singleness were diametrically opposed: I could have one or the other, but not both. And yet, I am more convinced than ever that not only are they compatible, but harmonious. Our aching reminds us we need to lean on God, and God reminds us we are relational beings like he is. You can desire marriage while still finding great contentment in your singleness.

In my darker moments with God, I felt like a dog being tricked. One of the things you're not supposed to do with dogs is offer them a treat and then never give it to them—it hurts their trust in you. When a person I thought I could have a romantic future with would appear in my life and then they would leave, or someone else would swoop in and marry them instead, I felt like the punchline of a massive cosmic joke: a dog foolish enough to keep reaching for the treats God offered me, only for him to yank them away time after time.

This perception I had of God created a deep distrust. I started wondering if God was either indifferent to my needs or incapable of acknowledging them. I questioned if God knew what was best for me, and I felt more alone than ever. Scripture says God loves us, and yet, so often we allow the lack of dates, the lack of eligible people, and the lack of a wedding band around our finger to dictate our opinion of God. We *acknowledge* God loves us without actually *believing* he does. While our longing for marriage is healthy, we can allow the ache within that longing to hurt our trust in God.

Contentedness isn't based on feeling satisfied—it's based on trust. And trust comes from relationship. Our relationship with Christ goes only as far as our ability to trust him with our lives. If we don't trust him, the pain we experience intensifies. Margaret Clarkson, who remained unmarried her entire life, talks about why this trust is crucial.

> [God] has promised to meet our needs and he honors his word. If we seek fulfillment in him, we shall find it. It may not be easy, but whoever said the Christian life was easy? The badge of Christ's discipleship is a cross.

> Why must I live my life alone? I do not know. But Jesus
> Christ is Lord of my life. I believe in the sovereignty of God,
> and I accept my singleness from his hand. He could have
> ordered my life otherwise, but he has not chosen to do so.
> As his child, I must trust his love and wisdom.[3]

We won't always understand God's plans, but we can trust
who he is and the plans he has for us. When we struggle with
where God has us, we fall back on our trust in him.

Barry is a single man, currently in his sixties, and knows
all too well the fears older singles tend to experience. Yet,
despite those fears, Barry urges us trust God:

> God knows you better than anybody else. He knows what
> your fit is, and he knows when that fit will come . . . Trust
> God. Trust your father to have your absolute best in mind,
> including in this arena . . . If you're not cultivating an
> actual relationship with Jesus . . . he's not going to be able
> to speak into [your desire] because you don't trust him. You
> don't trust somebody you don't know.[4]

In order to trust God, we need to know who he is—and
his character is most clearly evident in the person of Jesus
Christ. Jesus knows what you're going through, because he
went through what you're going through. "For we do not
have a high priest who is unable to sympathize with our
weaknesses, but one who in every respect has been tempted
as we are, yet without sin. Let us then with confidence draw
near . . . that we may receive mercy and find grace to help in
time of need" (Heb. 4:15-16). Christ has struggled in the
same ways we have. He was single and celibate his entire life.
There is no one who understands your suffering and your
deepest longings more.

Not only does God *understand* your longings, he *cares* about them, too. He gives us many small pleasures, even if we don't always realize it: the embrace from a gentle breeze, the taste of pleasurable food, the softness of carpet beneath bare feet, the sensation of a warm shower, the hug from a close friend. If God already blesses us in small ways, even when we don't acknowledge them, how much more can we trust him with the big desires we care about?

It's hard to know how to deal with our longings at times. They can linger on or regress, only to return full-force at unexpected moments. But, regardless of our struggles, regardless of our desires, God is primarily and chiefly concerned about us. He wants what is best for us, and what's best for us is, ultimately, a relationship with him.

God is a relational God, and Jesus clearly demonstrated this during his time on earth. Even when he was surrounded by crowds, he sought the individual. Whenever he performed miraculous healings, Jesus used touch to do so, even when the diseased person appeared untouchable. Dr. Paul Brand, who spent most of his life working with patients with leprosy, marvels at this personal aspect of Jesus.

> I have sometimes wondered why Jesus so frequently touched the people he healed, many of whom must have been unattractive, obviously diseased, unsanitary, smelly. With his power, he easily could have waved a magic wand. In fact, a wand would have reached more people than a touch . . . But he chose not to . . . He wanted those people, one by one, to feel his love and warmth and his full identification with them.[5]

Jesus showed affection to sinners, love toward those who had received none, and grace to those who hurt him. He loved and cared about the people around him, even when they didn't love him back.

Your ache does not go unnoticed. God cares about your love life. He cares about your deepest desires. When you ache, he aches with you. I would go so far as to say he cares far more than you do because he understands how you're wired even more than you do. We can trust him with our deepest yearnings.

Reflection Questions:

• Have you felt a deep emotional ache for intimacy? When have you felt it the most strongly? What do you wish you had that you feel a lack of in your singleness?

• God comforted Elijah both biologically, personally, and spiritually. What methods of comfort tend to help you the most in times of emotional distress or pain? What method tends to help you the least?

• Which areas of your life have you struggled to trust God with the most? What holds you back from giving them over to him? What has helped increase your trust in God?

14

TO DATE OR NOT TO DATE

In the years of college, there lived a man named Daniel. He had beside him a friend named Ava, with whom he had grown very close. She delighted in his company and saw potential for something more. But though Ava searched out Daniel's heart, he was not yet sure what to do about their friendship. So, Ava approached Daniel, saying, "What if we went on a double date and grabbed food or something with our friends?" Daniel pondered this in his heart.

And it became so.

Several days passed before the fateful night began. They traveled together—Daniel, Ava, and their friends—until they came to a place of food and wings. They talked amongst themselves, and there was much merriment. Daniel tried the wings and saw that they were pleasing to the lips and good for food. He looked to his friends and saw that their jokes were funny and their banter was effortless. These things delighted Daniel's heart, and he saw they were good.

As the moon grew higher in the sky, the friends returned to the campus from whence they came. Daniel and Ava found themselves in one of the lobbies, where they watched some movies Daniel had created in his younger years. Daniel saw that the movies were cringe, and they unsettled his soul. But

Ava had much enjoyment and teased Daniel to no end, and this made him happy. As the date ended, Daniel rested, full of joy and delight.

But there was another date, one whose outcome was far different.

In the days of high school, in the land of youth group, there was a girl named Rachel. Daniel found Rachel pleasing to the eye, and she found him the same. Rachel offered him the chance to go to a concert along with her and her friends. Daniel accepted, his heart glad, for he never had a chance to enjoy her company outside of youth group before.

So, Daniel traveled to the city of Chicago, by foot and by train, in the hopes of being with Rachel. Upon arriving at the concert, he met Rachel and her friends. Daniel noticed her friends were all men, and this troubled him. But Daniel also saw they were of friendly character, and this gave him some comfort. One of the men had a name which struck the hearts of those who heard it with awe (and, tragically, cannot be disclosed). He will be called Ryder.

As the concert began, a concern stirred within Daniel's heart. Rachel and Ryder were acting strange, staring into one another's eyes and holding hands, and Daniel grew worried that they were more than brother and sister in Christ. He pulled one of Rachel's friends aside, asking him the truth of the situation.

"I do not know," the friend said, "For she has had many a boyfriend." This greatly displeased Daniel's spirit. He saw that the concert's musicians had yet to perform and decided to return to his homeland before the appointed time.

Some days later, Daniel explained to Rachel what she had done to grieve him so. As he told her these things, Rachel responded, "When I said I liked you, I didn't mean it *that* way." This multiplied Daniel's anguish, and he returned home. And there was much weeping and gnashing of teeth.

GOING FROM "SINGLE" TO "DATING"

The world of dating can be wild and unpredictable. Some dates are exciting, as mine was with Ava, while others are deeply disappointing, as mine was with Rachel (none of these are their real names, by the way). Several articles describe modern dating using terms like "burnout" and "fatigue". Most stories online are nightmare stories of dates gone wrong, sudden betrayals, burned bridges, and unpaid dinners. One person described it as "death by a thousand cuts." This is profoundly sad, because dating should be thrilling and exciting. The Bible talks about the road to marriage as one of anticipation and joy. It's what the Song of Solomon is all about!

Why talk about dating in a book on singleness? We may not often think of it this way, but dating is a part of singleness. When you start dating, you don't stop being single. It's like how landing an interview for a job doesn't end your unemployment. But interviews can result in a job, and for this reason, they can be incredibly rewarding or incredibly discouraging.

Among Christians, one of our biggest headaches has less to do with singleness or dating and more with making the leap from one to the other. Few verses are more bewildering than the refrain to "not stir up or awaken love until it pleases" (Song 2:7). Great, but how will we know when it pleases?

I have some bad news for you: nothing can guarantee success in your dating life. The good news, however, is that while a lot of dating is outside of your control, there are some things you can do to better understand it and navigate it well. To that end, I've curated a series of questions to guide you through deciding whether to date someone or not.

Some of these may seem harsh, but these standards are in place for your spiritual flourishing. Standards also protect you from red herrings: people who are attractive but likely wouldn't work out. By having defined criteria, we can determine who is eligible to date a lot faster than if we had no standards in place.

1. DO THEY HAVE A RELATIONSHIP WITH JESUS?

This question comes first for a reason. Before figuring anything else out, you need to assess if your romantic prospect shares your faith.

Many people ignore this first step. In one survey, 77% of those interviewed said they would consider being in a committed relationship with someone of a different religion.[1] For us Christians, faith is non-negotiable. If marriage involves two people becoming one flesh, then we cannot bind ourselves to someone who shares a different spiritual allegiance. If you love God, then whoever you date needs to love him as well.

Paul stresses that we must "not be unequally yoked with unbelievers. For what partnership has righteousness with lawlessness? Or what fellowship has light with darkness?" (2

Cor. 6:14). One of the most important aspects of yoking oxen together was the pairing of the oxen themselves. If they didn't move at similar speeds, the faster ox would choke the other. Bonding yourself to someone at a very different place in their faith journey—or with a different worldview altogether—will lead to problems, not the least of which may include endangering your faith.

When God is our number one relationship, we need to ensure our second-highest relationship supports that. If you are serious about your relationship with God, then you need to be serious about dating those who want that relationship to flourish. Nonbelievers are off the table. Agnostics are off the table. People who say they're "religious" or "spiritual" are off the table. People who say they're Christian but act completely contrary to their faith are off the table.

It's tempting to believe that as long as you both respect each other's beliefs, everything will be fine, but the truth is that if someone doesn't have a relationship with Jesus, they will not value him in the same way you do. If Jesus is king over your life, that affects your values, your priorities, and your actions. If the person you're interested in has something else as king over their life, they will have different values, priorities, and life trajectory. Remember our discussion on having a foundation of rock for your marriage? If your spouse doesn't have Christ as their greatest relationship, you're building a house on top of sand.

Don't believe you can "date" someone to Jesus, either. If you are hoping to leverage your emotional proximity to someone in an attempt to change their worldview, you are engaging in deception at best and manipulation at worst.

Don't try to justify dating someone who doesn't share your faith by labeling it "ministry". Making friends with nonbelievers is simpler, cheaper, and much more honorable than going on dates with them. If they aren't serious about Christ, they aren't an option. Period.

Sometimes, you can't tell what a person believes right away. That's okay: it doesn't need to be the first question you ask everyone you meet, but it should be something you seek to determine as soon as possible.

2. IS GOD SAYING SOMETHING OTHER THAN "YES"?

If they have a relationship with Jesus, the next step is figuring out what God says about you dating this person in particular. We need to be cautious here, because many people wait to hear a "yes" from God instead of a "no." The problem is, when asking God for direct discernment, we can stay stuck in this stage if we're not careful. We wait for a "yes" and, then, if we don't hear a response, we interpret it as God not having given an answer; and this brings everything to a standstill.

If we wait to hear *anything* from God, we may not be prepared to hear nothing. The thing is, silence is a possible response from God. If he *does* speak, his answer isn't always immediately clear. Or, if it is, we may ignore it anyway. In my experience, a "no" from God is clearer and more quickly heard than a "yes." When a traffic light stays green, no change is necessary. However, when it turns yellow or red, we need to apply the brakes and alter our trajectory.

If someone asks you out on a date and you aren't sure, do not, under any circumstances, use prayer as an excuse to avoid hard conversations. Many people I know have played the "God Card" to justify ending conversations with someone they don't like, using God as a shield to deflect honesty.

Saying things like "let me pray about it" isn't bad, unless you're saying it with no intention of giving an answer. If you tell the person you intend on praying, be sure to clarify with them how long you intend to pray for: a few days, a week, etc. If you say you'll pray about it with no intention of ever having a follow-up conversation, you're wasting their time and playing with their feelings.

Some of us pray out of fear in a different way: we're worried that the person may not be the person God has for us to marry. Fear not: so long as you seek him, nothing you do can compromise or undo the work of God. "For I know the plans I have for you, declares the Lord, plans for welfare and not for evil, to give you a future and a hope" (Jer. 29:11). God proclaimed this to the people of Israel, who were in captivity at the time. His plans didn't match their circumstances, but they had to place their hope in him, not themselves. We must do the same, praying like the psalmist who wrote, "Show me your ways, Lord, teach me your paths. Guide me in your truth and teach me, for you are God my Savior, and my hope is in you all day long" (Ps. 25:4-5 NIV).

Finally—and this should be obvious—whatever you hear from the Lord, do it. If he isn't telling you to avoid or delay pursuing this person, then our next step is to assess ourselves.

3. WHAT DO OTHERS THINK?

I've already touched on this in the "Friends Wanted" chapter, but it's worth reinforcing: be sure to seek insight from people you trust throughout this process. Do they know this person? Are they familiar with the person's reputation? Boaz is attracted to Ruth in part because he had heard of her good deeds (Ruth 2:10-12). In the Song of Solomon, the bride says to her husband, "your name is oil poured out" (Song 1:3). He has a good name, a good reputation. See if the person you are interested in has a good name and good character that is already known by others. If you meet them online, see to it you create room for others to help you discern as you date.

It bears repeating: your friends are one of the greatest blessings in your dating process. If they know the person you're interested in, they may be able to speak wisdom and insight into whether they are actually as great as they seem—or as well matched as you think. If they don't already know the person, they can still provide valuable perspective should things take off.

Chances are you know someone who started dating and then disappeared off the face of the earth. If things work out between you and this person, don't do that. Lean into your community. Remember, even if you're dating someone, you're still single. Maintain your friendships regardless of your dating status.

That said, you can also listen to what others have to say too much. Several times in my own life, I've had friends try and set me up with a woman they thought was incredible but whom I wasn't as excited about. In these situations, I would doubt my own intuition: "I'm not that crazy about this person, but if everyone else says she's great, then perhaps something is wrong with how I'm seeing her." If that's how you're feeling, don't go for it. I wouldn't want someone to pursue me because they feel pressured to, and neither should you do the same to someone else. At the same time, there might be wisdom in leaning into your friends' advice, so proceed thoughtfully. Romance should be natural, not forced.

4. DOES MAKING A MOVE CHANGE YOUR MIND?

One time, at a local festival, I stumbled across an almond butter stand; and I couldn't help but notice how attractive the girl running it was. She was charming, and her personality really seemed to click with mine. I thought about going up to her to have a more intentional conversation, but I hesitated. I was anxious about what might happen. I ran through all the scenarios in my head and decided to just go for it. I walked up to her and we began to chat. She asked me what I did for a living. I was working for a church at the time, and after telling her this, I asked if she went to church often.

"Not much," she replied, "Only during Christmas and Easter."

Right there, I got my clarity. She wasn't active in the church, something I wanted my future wife to have. I walked away from that interaction feeling good. The "what if" in my mind was answered, and the stress went away. God didn't tell me about the girl before I took the step: he moved naturally through our conversation.

Theodore Roosevelt is often credited as saying, "In any moment of decision, the best thing you can do is the right thing, the next best thing is the wrong thing, and the worst thing you can do is nothing." At some point, you need to take a step and go for it.

God often provides the most clarity once we take action. One example of this is when Abraham and Lot decide to split the land between their two clans. After their decision, God reaffirms his promise to Abraham to prosper him and give him all the land he sees (Gen. 13:8-18).

Sometimes, God won't make things clear until you take a step forward. This could look like telling the person how you feel about them, or it could look like asking them on a date and seeing how they respond. While that can feel stress-inducing, so long as you prioritize your relationship with him, he will be right beside you every step of the way.

There are, of course, exceptions. If you feel you need more clarity or have felt stress even after securing a date with someone, then jumping into something may not be the best choice. For me, the latter was true. I would date women out of a place of self-medication, and I didn't realize this fact until years later. Not succumbing to my own self-imposed pressure would have saved me a lot of stress in dating.

Should the man be the one to ask the woman out? It's a question that seems easier to answer than to practice. In fact, as one pastor observed, both genders are likely to place responsibility on the other to ask them out.[2] I'll touch on this briefly, though it warrants more thorough discussion. While many believe men should ask the women out, *anyone* can show or share romantic interest.

For women, podcaster Kait Tomlin suggests "dropping the hanky." Back in the Victorian era, women would show a man they were interested by looking them in the eye and dropping their handkerchief in front of them. This would indirectly signal "Hey, I'm interested in you. Come talk to me." As Kait is quick to disclaim, "dropping the hanky does not mean you are planning the date, okay? It doesn't mean that you're, like, 'hey, do you want to go on a date with me?' It's you opening the door. It's you giving the guy a green light."[3]

5. DOES ALL OF YOU WANT THIS PERSON?

"Um, duh," I hear you saying, "That's why I'm considering a date with them in the first place!" But there is a distinction between finding someone good-looking and being drawn to who they are. Attraction is good, but it isn't enough to build a relationship on. I've lived in large cities, rural farmland, and just about everything in-between. Trust me, there will be attractive people wherever you go. Instead, look deeper. Look for character.

One tool that's helped me discern this is to assess if my body, mind, heart, and soul are in agreement about the person. This can work whether you're dating them or considering a date with them. When we take note of how our bodies react around them, how we feel during our interactions with them, and how compatible our relationship with God is to theirs, it can help us determine if they are a good fit or not. Let's break each of these down.

BODY: Yes, you should feel physically attracted to this person, but this category isn't just about sexual desire; it's also about your bodily needs. Depending on who you are and what your love language is, this will vary. I value spending time with those I'm close to, so I want someone who desires to be physically with me, who initiates spending time together. Overall, your bodily needs aren't mental or emotional, but physical. How do you feel when the person is around you? Do you tense up with anxiety, or are you thrilled to be with them? What physical, non-erotic needs are you looking for in a relationship?

MIND: This has to do with your personalities and how well they interact with each other. Is conversation effortless with this person? Do you enjoy hanging out with them? Of course you will have your differences, but do you feel like they "get" you, as in understand what you're trying to say without much explanation or justification? Are you invested in this person and the trajectory of their life?

HEART: This is where your emotions are important to consider. Do you feel like yourself around this person? Pay attention to the emotional "fruit" that is produced when you interact with them: do you feel a sense of joy and peace around them? If you are pursuing this person because you feel you *have to* (or are trying to make it work) and not because you *want to*, then dating can quickly burn you out. If you feel anxious around this person, that can be another bad sign.

SOUL: This isn't just about sharing the same faith, but also how they live out and practice their faith. If you don't know this person well, then dating will provide you the space to learn whether or not you share beliefs on important theological topics. Right now, it's about assessing their attitude toward Christ. Is it clear they have put thought into their faith? Do they navigate the complexities of life or difficult questions with wisdom? Are they excited and invested in the work God is doing in other people?

In my experience, it's harder to say "no" when someone is compatible in two or three of these categories, but we need to look for someone who is compatible with all four. If there is a girl who is attractive, loves being around you, and really clicks with you but doesn't have an intentional faith, then she is compatible with your mind, body, and heart, but not your soul. If a guy is passionate about his relationship with God and empathizes with you well, but isn't that attractive and doesn't make a lot of time for you, then he is compatible with your mind, heart, and soul, but not your body. Use these four categories as a guide, but discern well on your own. You will likely have different ideas of what these categories look like than I do.

Overall, you want to avoid dating someone out of self-medication, obligation, despair, or compromise. When you find someone who agrees with your body, mind, heart, and soul, the question goes from "what if" to "what's next?"

AWAKENING LOVE

There's nothing inherently magical or life-changing about going on a date. It can certainly *feel* magical, but a date is effectively hanging out with a purpose. And that's all it should be. You won't get married after one date or two (at least I hope not!). Take your time and run at a pace you are comfortable with. Your closest friendships weren't made overnight, and neither will your marriage. It takes time and effort to know someone well.

Dating with standards is a lot like bowling. Similar to a bowling lane, dating has a start and an end goal. Just as you finish bowling once the ball hits the pins, so too do you finish dating when you decide to marry the person or end the relationship. There should be a natural momentum when you're with this person, a joy and peace when you're around them. They should bring out in you a person you enjoy.

Biblical standards are necessary, but they are like guardrails in a bowling lane: healthy limitations that, so long as your relationship says within them, ensure success. But when we overthink, we grab the bowling ball and drag it along the lane floor, manually moving it toward the pins. The movement isn't natural, it's forced. Instead, you need to release the ball, letting God and your guardrails guide its direction. If you're constantly looking for boxes on your list to check off, you're in the wrong headspace. Just let the bowling ball roll.

Trust that your romantic love will awaken in its proper time, not by prying open its eyes but by the natural waking of genuine connection to another human being. When you are patient and walk in step with God, you will find your love life won't just survive, but flourish.

Reflection Questions:

• How would you describe your dating life in a single word? Do you wish you could use a different word instead? What word would that be?

• Review the five questions listed in this chapter. Which of these seem the most helpful? Are there any you struggle with implementing?

• What would it look like for someone to be compatible with your body, mind, heart, and soul? What are your needs in those areas?

15

NINE WAYS TO BECOME IRRESISTIBLE

Our culture has a strong fascination with dating. You don't see headlines such as "How To Spice Up Your Celibacy" or "Dating the Lord: Five Fun Ideas for Time With the Creator". Rather, we are inundated with "How to Win the Girl of Your Dreams" and "Date Nights He'll Never Forget". It is dating, more than singleness or marriage, that enjoys the biggest spotlight from society.

But dating can also be incredibly confusing. The way we date has changed over a very short time period. Back in the day, parents played a significant role in selecting your spouse. Then, it became courtship. Then "going steady". Then casual dating and hook-up culture. Now, it's dating apps. Over the next couple decades, the landscape of dating will likely change again.

Scripture doesn't specifically mention dating, either. There aren't any verses like, "Then the Lord said onto Mary, 'Send not the D.M. unto him'" or "Thou shalt not ghost thine neighbor." But the world of dating is volatile. The words and definitions we use for it change frequently. The Bible doesn't address specific *methods* of dating because it focuses on something deeper: the *function* of dating.

In the last chapter, I gave a basic framework for making a decision on whether to date or not. Now, I want to outline tools we can use to guide us through dating relationships. If I outlined an exact method, this chapter would age like milk. The *function* of dating, however, has remained unchanged. I love how Ben Stuart describes it:

> It is important to note that dating is a process. I keep coming around to that word because a process has movement to it. It's a series of actions unto a predetermined end. Dating is not a status that you sit in without any kind of momentum. You shouldn't . . . just hang out there indefinitely. It's meant to have movement to an end—a destination called marriage.[1]

We could substitute dating for any other method, be it courtship or online DMs or blind dates or even arranged marriages, but the purpose would be the same: a process to bring you and a compatible person together for marriage. Scripture may not contain a list of the top ten dating apps the Israelites used, but it has much to say on finding a godly spouse.

Scripture enables us to "walk in a manner worthy of the Lord, fully pleasing to him: bearing fruit in every good work and increasing in the knowledge of God" (Col. 1:10). This applies to everything we do, including dating.

Only healthy trees can bear fruit. Trees that are weak or diseased either bear fruit of poor quality or no fruit at all. Thus, your fruit points to the health of your roots. Paul provides a practical list of the "good fruit" we should seek to cultivate: "the fruit of the Spirit is love, joy, peace, patience, kindness, goodness, faithfulness, gentleness, self-control"

(Gal. 5:22-23). If you prioritize Christ in your life, that choice shows through the decisions you make, the interactions you have with others, and the areas you direct your time and resources.

We seldom consider what bearing good fruit looks like when we date, but Marshall Segal emphasizes its importance.

> Follow all the fruits of the Spirit down to the root of your
> sin, whatever your besetting sins, and find victory while
> you're still single. It will prepare you to date well now, and
> it will serve your future marriage and ministry in ways you
> cannot even comprehend.[2]

When properly applied, the fruit of the Spirit provides us with a framework for not only dating well—how we should seek to behave—but also for evaluating the person we are dating and our compatibility with them.

And so, based on the verse in Galatians, the rest of this chapter analyzes each fruit within the context of dating. In each section, I've included questions designed to help in evaluating the fruit of the person you're dating, as well as the fruits dating them brings out in you. This will aid you both in discerning the health of your relationship and dating from hearts with healthy roots.

LOVE

A popular assumption is that love is a feeling. We often date or enter into marriage, with the unspoken assumption that if we love them, the person we're with should always make us feel happy and fulfilled. However, love isn't fundamentally a feeling—it's a choice. Choosing to love someone may make you feel good as a result, but the feeling should be neither the motivation nor the goal. Marriage counselor Gary Chapman explores this idea:

> For some of us . . . We go against our feelings and get out of bed. Why? Because we believe there is something worthwhile to do that day. And normally, before the day is over, we feel good about having gotten up. Our actions preceded our emotions. The same is true with love.[3]

Feelings come and go. If our love is based on emotions, then relationships will only last as long as the feeling does. But biblical love is steadfast and unconditional. Once you become one flesh in marriage, you are committing to love each other—to choose each other—when it's easy and when it's hard. Jesus said, "You did not choose me, but I chose you and appointed you that you should go and bear fruit" (John 15:16). No one loves more than God because God *is* love.

There's a reason love is the first of the Fruit of the Spirit: it's the most foundational and the most important. Choosing each other is the essence of love and marriage.

In dating, you are deciding whether you want to spend the rest of your lives together. Given this, dating isn't so much about choosing the other person as it is considering the decision to choose them every day for the rest of your life. Because of this, watch how the other person acts. Watch what and who they choose to put first. If they add conditions to their love ("if you want me to love you more, I'm going to need you to . . ."), then it isn't the love of Christ.

I had a mentor who observed, "In any relationship, the person with the most power is the one who cares the least about it." Make sure you are equally invested in each other, and that the investment deepens over time.

Questions to consider love: When you need love, is God where you first seek it from? Is there anything or anyone you or the person you're dating are regularly loving above God? Is choosing to love the person you're dating worthwhile or burdensome? Do they make excuses when they act unloving, or do they apologize sincerely?

JOY

Describing love as a choice can make relationships sound like they will be lifeless and hollow. In actuality, the opposite is true. Scripture urges married men to "rejoice in the wife of your youth" (Prov. 5:18). When he first encounters Eve, Adam's first words are those of delight: "This at last is bone of my bones and flesh of my flesh!" (Gen. 2:23). Joy is an inherent part of marriage and romance.

The *choice* of love is its foundation, but *joy* is its shape. There will be times where you don't delight in your spouse, but by choosing to love them anyway, joy will eventually come back.

Tragically, joy can be lost in the dating process. Couples that have dated each other for years can continue to stay together not out of joy, but out of obligation. Their thoughts may go something like this:

"I don't know how I feel about us, but she says we're meant to be together."

"We've been together this long, might as well keep going."

"I can't leave him: who else would he go to for support?"

This kind of thinking saps joy from dating. Don't decide to date solely because you're already close friends or because they're a strong believer and "it just makes sense". When you try to "tough it out" in dating, you are treating it like a marriage instead of an evaluation.

If there is no joy in your dating process, there won't be any in your marriage, either. You should have chemistry with each other and miss one another when you're apart. They should bring out a version of you that you enjoy.

I saw this in one of my friends, James. He had dated other women, but when he met Sarah, the woman he eventually married, I saw the effect it had on him. Whenever they were together, she brought out more of his humor and his passion for God. Her presence brought out *more* of the friend I loved. She didn't change him; her presence simply brought out different sides of him I hadn't seen before. I want that for you and your relationships.

Questions to consider joy: Do you look forward to spending time with the person you're dating? Do you like the person you become when you're around them? Do you feel a sense of obligation or resentment toward the person, or are you genuinely excited to be with them?

PEACE

Just because you're dating someone you delight in (and who delights in you) doesn't mean life is going to be puppies and rainbows from here on out. There are going to be storms and immense difficulties. Peace is what carries you through those times.

Peace isn't a default setting: it's something we need to chase after. "Turn away from evil and do good; seek peace and pursue it" (Ps. 34:14). Most of us probably don't consciously pursue God's peace. Why? Because peace fights against our human desire for certainty and control.

Peace comes from our trust in God and his plans for us. Describing a godly wife, Proverbs says "Strength and dignity are her clothing, and she laughs at the time to come" (Prov. 31:25). She is not ruled by anxiety and her actions are not dictated by hesitation: she is so confident and sure of her steps that it's as obvious as her clothing. You want a person who embodies that and brings that out in you.

Look at how the person you're dating handles conflict and uncertainty. Do small, unexpected obstacles send them spiraling? Are they unable to handle everyday situations when you're not around? If they can't handle what life throws their way, then you'll need to shoulder their life's craziness on top of yours in marriage. People will always face difficulties, but it's easier to face it together than for one of you to carry it on your own.

There will be stressful moments, but you should generally feel peace when you're with the person you're dating. If you're constantly feeling anxious around them, you should seriously reevaluate the relationship dynamic.

Questions to consider peace: Do you usually feel peace around the person you're with? How do they handle stressful situations? Do they seek to establish peace when conflict arises? Are you confident in both of your abilities to handle conflict and crises well? Is the person actively looking to resolve conflicts or confusion?

PATIENCE

The Song of Solomon is undoubtedly the steamiest, most sensual book in the entire Bible. It's about a man and woman about to be married, and boy oh boy, do they want each other. And yet, there's a refrain. "I charge you by the gazelles and by the does of the field: Do not arouse or awaken love until it so desires" (Song 2:7 NIV).

One does not rush to a gazelle or a deer. To aggressively approach them would risk harming you both. Instead, you must approach carefully and slowly. This is where patience comes into play: it informs the pace of the dating process. Often, when dating someone, you will have different expectations about showing affection, about when you feel you can trust each other, about what kind of marriage you want to have, and so on. One of you might feel more confident in your relationship than the other. Handling these situations well will require patience.

One of the greatest challenges we face is learning to wait well, especially when you aren't sure what the outcome will be. It goes back to trusting God. Sometimes, we can act out of romantic desire prematurely. Be careful in your approach to dating, and don't push the person you desire into a place they're uncomfortable with.

Patience is essential when it comes to conflict. We are all sinners in recovery. As you date, there will be past trauma and baggage that you will have to deal with in the relationship. There will be moments when your partner will hurt you, even unintentionally. Your response to these moments must not be done hastily.

"A hot-tempered man stirs up strife, but he who is slow to anger quiets contention" (Prov. 15:18). Whenever someone is patient in conflict, they look past their own defensiveness and seek to understand the other side. When you face disagreements in dating, watch how they deal with the conflict.

It's also important to watch how they wait, whether it's hearing back from you, unexpected traffic delays, or sexual boundaries. Waiting doesn't go away when you get married; it just takes on different forms.

Questions to consider patience: Do you find yourself or your partner getting easily angered about something specific? Do they seek to understand you whenever you disagree with them? Do you engage patiently and carefully with each other when something doesn't go your way?

KINDNESS

If patience is how we passively respond to someone, then kindness is how we actively engage with them. Anyone can claim to love God, but watch how they treat those around them. Kindness shouldn't be reserved for those they have a crush on. Observe how they treat their family and how they talk about their exes. Listen to what they say to waiters or cashiers. Note how they deal with people who hurt them. This is more than being nice, it's about incorporating grace and mercy into how we deal with the world, ourselves, and others.

Kindness also looks like honesty. After all, "clarity is kindness". Proverbs says "an honest answer kisses the lips" (Prov. 24:26). So much of the confusion experienced in dating can be boiled down to a lack of clarity. This isn't "tough love" or "telling it as it is", this is telling the truth in a loving way that respects the person and wants their best. This means being transparent about your expectations, how you feel about the other person, and where you are in the relationship, whether on the first date or the tenth. If you're asking them out, call it a date. "We should hang out sometime" communicates nothing. If you want to end the relationship, say it gently but clearly. Don't just ghost them and hope they get the hint.

Some of us are guilty of using God as a scapegoat instead of being honest about our feelings. There are infamous breakups where the initiator says, "I feel like God is moving me away from this relationship". In other words, "I'm too scared to own up to my feelings, so I'm going to let God take the blame for the pain I'm causing you." Don't bring God into this. He's not ending this, you are. Take responsibility for your actions. Even if God *is* telling you, you're the one choosing to listen and follow through on what he's saying. Taking ownership of your role is part of being kind.

Make sure your standards for your love life are kind as well. Some of us, especially those who have been hurt in relationships before, can set standards that are unattainable or perfectionistic. Prayerfully think through what you are asking of someone in your relationship. Is the list you have for them kind?

Questions to consider kindness: How does your partner treat their exes, their friends, or their family? Are you honest with them about where you are and how you're feeling? Are your standards for them kind?

GOODNESS

Goodness can often be confused with kindness. The way I distinguish the two is this: kindness is the external expression, while goodness is the fuel that motivates it. We practice goodness by seeing others the way that God sees them and recognizing their value. Goodness is not about reflecting the perfection of God, it is about reflecting the *character* of God. In dating, this looks like honoring and being genuinely invested in the person you're in a relationship with. Whatever you do, whether in the date or in the breakup, your actions must come from a place of goodness, a strong desire to see that person flourish under God.

You are dating royalty. We must treat each other as sons and daughters of the King. If I tell people I respect women and then proceed to chase after a woman who told me she isn't interested, I am not respecting her wishes. "The Lord is good, a stronghold in the day of trouble; he knows those who take refuge in him" (Nahum 1:7). In the presence of goodness, there is security and safety. A person whose goodness is like God's is someone around whom we feel comfortable and free to be ourselves.

Our goodness should mirror the goodness of God. Ergo, there should be a consistency to it: we should live lives of integrity. In dating, this means not misleading the other person or playing games.

I made a huge blunder in this area. I told a girl I liked her, and we began intentionally talking. Although she was great, I felt a tremendous amount of anxiety about the situation. I ended things with her a few weeks later. Then, I started second-guessing my decision, so I reached out to her again. She agreed to give me another chance. The anxiety returned, and a week after we got back together, I ended things a second time. Learn from my mistake and *don't* do what I did. Don't force yourself to stick with someone you don't feel good about. It will end up confusing and hurting both of you.

Goodness should also inform how we deal with each other's emotional baggage. "An excellent wife is the crown of her husband, but she who brings shame is like rottenness in his bones" (Prov. 12:4). God doesn't shame us for being sinners, and neither should we shame the other person for their shortcomings. I've seen hurt men and women, but especially women, do this to the opposite gender. But, as one female podcaster said, "No matter what you feel about men, how you talk about men matters."[4] Our words and actions matter. The net result of other people's encounters with us should point them toward Christ.

"Beloved, do not imitate evil but imitate good. Whoever does good is from God; whoever does evil has not seen God" (3 John 11). Good does not come naturally to us, it comes from imitating God's goodness. Our lives, and the decisions we make therein, should point others to Christ. The goal should be the same: to have that person be better for having been in your presence, whether your relationship ends in a break-up or in marriage.

Questions to consider goodness: Are the people you've romantically pursued better for having come into contact with you? Does the person you're dating live a life that imitates Christ? Do they have a low tolerance of sin in their own life? Are they willing to deal with your baggage and stick it out with you?

FAITHFULNESS

Some spiritual fruit is harder to detect in the moment. Faithfulness is one of these. It becomes more apparent over time, especially in dating. Not only does it refer to faith in God, it also refers to a steadfastness of character, a willingness to uphold commitments.

In the previous chapter I made my point about Christians only dating Christians, so I'll make this brief: our faith affects our priorities. Being faithful to God means a reverence for and obedience to his word above all else. As you date, watch the person's actions and decision-making. Is God's truth negotiable to them? Do they carry out God's will, even if it goes against what they want? There is a significant difference between those who seek romance on their terms, and those who seek it on God's.

But faithfulness is also demonstrated through the other commitments one has in their life. How the person you date treats the other relationships in their life will almost directly correlate to their relationship with you. Watch your partner's relationships with their friends and family. This is how Isaac meets his wife, Rebekah. She is watering her camels and sees his servant's camels are thirsty, so she goes out her way to water them (Gen. 24:10-20). She isn't aware that her work is for any romantic interest, she is simply doing it out of her own heart.

Get to know your partner's community. If they don't have one, that's a concern. Without other relationships in their life, not only does it make the person harder to evaluate, but it's a red flag if they don't have a community they're leaning on. Their social life and faith life are *their* responsibility, not yours. On the other hand, if they want to know *your* community and the people that matter to you, that's a green flag in my book. I'll never forget the sexiest thing a woman ever said to me as we were dating: "Daniel, don't take this the wrong way: I love spending time with you, but I also want to meet your friends, as well."

Questions to consider faithfulness: Do your actions in the relationship match your feelings and values about it? If you were to mute the person you're dating, would their actions still reflect their faith? Are they trustworthy? Are they loyal to the people they love? Do they have a life outside of your relationship? Are they interested in getting to know your friends?

GENTLENESS

While faithfulness is one's relationship to what God has placed in their life, gentleness is one's relationship to conflict. Instead of asserting their will, a gentle person listens before taking action. They are receptive to feedback and open to criticism. In writing to Titus, Paul advises his congregants "to be submissive to rulers and authorities, to be obedient, to be ready for every good work, to speak evil of no one, to avoid quarreling, to be gentle, and to show perfect courtesy toward all people." (Titus 3:1-2).

Gentleness is not the absence of conflict. Rather, it affects how we engage with it. In a dating relationship, every action should be done gently and humbly—whether it's telling someone that you like them, how you interact with them, or how the relationship is ended. Watch how they respond to antagonism, to feedback, to correction, and see if they change their behavior according to that correction or not. We should not shy away from the truth, but our gentleness dictates how the truth is presented to others. We must be tender and merciful without compromising the Word of God or the facts of the situation.

One beautiful example of gentleness is in the book of Ruth. The way Ruth asks for Boaz to marry her is incredibly gentle and respectful: she doesn't victimize herself and desperately plead for help. Instead, she humbles herself and throws herself at his feet, literally (Ruth 3:6-9). She is honest about her interest in him. She doesn't pressure Boaz or shame him, and he doesn't do either of those in his response to her, either. Women, especially widows, had low social standing in the day. If Boaz had shamed Ruth or forced his kinsman-redeemer status over her, it would have been typical of the day for him to do so. But he doesn't. He empowers and honors her in kind.

In your dating life, how can you seek to honor someone, even someone that you aren't interested in? When we are humble and gentle, it doesn't mean we agree with everyone else or run from conflict. Instead, it means we focus on restoration and honor above all things. Jesus encourages us, "Take my yoke upon you, and learn from me, for I am gentle and lowly in heart, and you will find rest for your souls" (Matt. 11:29). Through the gentleness of Jesus, we find rest.

Questions to consider gentleness: When you are wronged by someone, what is your first response? When you describe past girlfriends or boyfriends, what words do you use? Do you listen well? Do you seek to honor the other person, even when you disagree with them? Do they treat you like a child of God, or like a burden or accessory?

SELF-CONTROL

Self-control is the ability to deny the fulfillment of our desires when doing so is ultimately better for us. It's not wrong to have desires, but it's wrong to place the fulfillment of those desires above all else. As Jesus says, "If anyone would come after me, let him deny himself and take up his cross and follow me" (Matt. 16:24-25). When we run toward Jesus, self-control is required.

Proverbs warns, "A man without self-control is like a city broken into and left without walls" (Prov. 25:28). A city without walls has no boundaries and there is no safety. Someone who lacks self-control is similar. They are fundamentally self-serving: their allegiance is, first and foremost, to their immediate desires. You don't want to date someone like that. If they don't have boundaries for themselves, they won't respect yours.

One area where most singles struggle with self-control is in sexuality. If both of you are attracted to each other (which you should be), crossing sexual boundaries seems natural, even normal. But sex was designed by God to keep two people together in marriage. In dating, you need to remember that you aren't married. No matter how serious the relationship is or how long it has lasted, you are not bound to each other. If you are dating someone toxic or abusive, get out of the relationship immediately.

I've never met a couple that regretted having too many boundaries. Establish boundaries and encourage each other in reinforcing them. This isn't a one-time conversation, but a continuous dialogue. By practicing self-control, you are placing God's will and God's desires above your own. Marriage and singleness were made as separate gifts, and self-control is a habit that will bless both.

Self-control can also be seen in other ways. It can be seen when someone is cut off in traffic, and they bite their tongue from saying something in anger. It's found in discipline when they stayed up late at night but forced themselves to get out of bed and go to church the next morning. When their focus is on long-term priorities instead of short-term gratification, that's self-control. That's the spouse you want.

Questions to consider self-control: How do you invite God into your weaknesses? What areas of self-control do you struggle with, and what can you do to improve those areas? What is your definition of "going too far" in a relationship? Which locations or times of day are harder for you to resist temptation?

• • •

Paul doesn't refer to these as the "fruits" of the Spirit, but as a collective "fruit" of the Spirit. He assumes these are all displayed at the same time, not separately. They are all interlinked. If you fall short of being kind, you will be less patient and less loving, as well. If a girl dates a guy who tries pushing her boundaries sexually, he isn't only weak in the area of self-control, he is showing impatience with the dating process, a lack of kindness to the woman he is dating, and so on. When one seed becomes moldy, the whole fruit is rotten.

it's not about nitpicking each fruit so much as it is seeing evidence of the Fruit more broadly in someone's else.

However, before we evaluate others, we must first evaluate ourselves. Yes, you should avoid dating unhealthy people who don't display good fruit, but you also need to be a healthy person for other people to date. As Nancy Wilson makes clear:

> If you want God to provide you with a husband, you have
> to consider whether you are the kind of woman that the
> kind of man you want to marry would want to marry. Shall
> I go over that again? What kind of woman is that kind of
> man looking for? Are you that kind of woman?[5]

Dating in the Christian world is hard, and searching for an unmarried believer who is serious about their faith makes the process ten times harder. Dating can be discouraging, but our posture toward dating can affect the way we engage with it.

Fruit isn't just grown: it spreads. It contains seeds which grow more fruit, and it tastes sweet and blesses those who receive it. So, as you look at your faith and the way you are pursuing romance, what fruit are you currently bearing?

Reflection Questions:

• Before reading this chapter, what standards would you use to determine whether the relationship you were in was healthy? Are they helpful to you?

• Can you identify healthy fruit in dates or relationships you've had before? What has unhealthy or harmful fruit looked like?

• Of all the fruits mentioned, which one is the easiest for you to live out? Which one is the most difficult?

CONCLUSION

THE TALENT OF BEING UNMARRIED

One of my biggest spiritual blunders happened at a high school retreat. The worship team was playing, and I felt the Spirit prompt me to pray with a guy who was new to our small group. But he wasn't someone I was fond of: he seemed arrogant and cocky. So, I did the most God-honoring thing imaginable . . .

I said "no".

Later that night in my small group, I learned that, several minutes after I said "no" to God, he prompted my small group leader to pray for the same guy. Unlike me, the leader said "yes", and through that prayer the guy ended up accepting Jesus that very night.

We all have our reasons for saying "no" to God. It might be someone we'd rather avoid than confront. It could include taking a step we feel unqualified for. We may think that we need more time. The reality is this: one way or another, God's will is going to be done. He doesn't ask us to carry it out because he's reliant on our obedience. He does so because he is inviting us to play a part in what he is doing in the world. God never thinks to himself, "She'd better not mess up my calling, otherwise, I don't know what I'm going to do" or "If he says 'no', I'm not sure how this is going to work." God doesn't need you; he wants you. In my case, he invited me to play a part in his work, I said no, and so he invited someone else. God's will was still done, the only difference is that I missed a chance to be a part of it.

I don't want you to say "no" to God in your singleness. God doesn't care about your income, your education level, or even your scriptural knowledge. All that matters is your receptivity to the Lord. What matters is saying "yes" to what God gives you.

God doesn't wait for people to be "ready"; he simply makes ready those who listen to him. He wanted Moses to speak to Pharaoh, the most powerful man in the world at the time, in spite of Moses' speech impediment (Ex. 4:10-17). He chose Jonah to minister to the city of Nineveh, despite Jonah wanting the people in it to perish (Jonah 3:10-4:4). God will use your skills and your abilities—or lack thereof. No matter how ill-equipped or unprepared you feel, it won't stop him from using you.

Your singleness, however long it lasts, is a gift. And God doesn't give without purpose. Peter explains that "as each has received a gift, use it to serve one another, as good stewards of God's varied grace . . . in order that in everything God may be glorified through Jesus Christ" (1 Peter 4:10-11).

When God gives us a gift, he trusts us to use it in a manner that gives him the glory. This is what it means to steward the gifts we have received. Throughout scripture, God will freely give a blessing and then ask that a portion of it be faithfully returned to him. For the time on this earth God has given us, he asks for the Sabbath (Lev. 23:3). For the money he has given to us—no matter what amount—he has asked that we tithe some of it back to him (Lev. 27:30, Prov. 3:9). In moments of drawing closer to God, we fast: choosing, for a time, to give back the blessing of food (Ezra 8:21-23). By returning to God a portion of what we receive, we demonstrate our trust in his provision.

God also uses our faithful stewardship to bless others in turn. We see this when he tells Abram "I will make of you a great nation, and I will bless you and make your name great, so that you will be a blessing" (Gen. 12:2). God wasn't just blessing Abram, he was blessing him so Abram could be a blessing to others.

As struggling romantics, we typically don't think about singleness as a blessing, much less a means of blessing others. We usually see it as a season to survive, rather than a season in which we can thrive. But God has blessed you with the gift of singleness and intends to bring great good through that gift—both for you and for the people around you. The only question is, will you accept it? Will you answer his call?

BURYING THE TALENT

At the first job I ever had, one of my coworkers smoked cigarettes. He knew they were unhealthy, but didn't seem concerned about it. He told me, "I'll just quit when I'm older, I've got plenty of time." He didn't think his actions had consequences and assumed that everything could be fixed the moment he wanted them to be.

We do this in our faith, too. We put off tithing and say, "I'll do that once I have more money." We ignore the Sabbath and say, "I'll do that once I have more time." We neglect a relationship with Jesus and say, "I'll worry about that once I'm older and more religious." We assume we have plenty of time to change our ways and put aside long-term worries for later. But God doesn't want us someday—he wants us now. As we've discussed, singleness is a gift, and we need to learn how to steward it well.

There's a parable Jesus tells that paints a vivid picture of what it looks like to steward our gifts well. It's about a master who entrusts his servants with varying sums of money: to one servant he gives five talents, to another two, and to the third he gives one. Talents were an incredible amount of money: one talent was equivalent to about six thousand days of labor.

After some time, the master returns and assesses what his servants did with the talents given to them. The one who had five talents reveals he made five more, and the master says, "Well done, good and faithful servant. You have been faithful over a little; I will set you over much. Enter into the joy of your master." (Matt. 25:21). The servant who had two talents shares he made two more, and the master affirms him in the same way. The servant with the one talent, however, was not quite as fruitful. Fearing his master, he did nothing with his talent and buried it in the ground.

> But his master answered him, "You wicked and slothful servant! You knew that I reap where I have not sown and gather where I scattered no seed? Then you ought to have invested my money with the bankers, and at my coming I should have received what was my own with interest. So take the talent from him and give it to him who has the ten talents. For to everyone who has will more be given, and he will have an abundance. But from the one who has not, even what he has will be taken away. And cast the

worthless servant into the outer darkness. In that place there will be weeping and gnashing of teeth."

(Matt. 25:26-30)

It can be easy to interpret the master's reaction as overly harsh. My initial response is to sympathize with the third servant and make excuses for him: he was scared of his master, had anxiety about the responsibility given to him, didn't feel qualified, and so on. But the wicked servant wasn't given an impossible task: he failed to do with one talent what his colleagues did with much more.

As we look deeper into this text, we need to consider this parable from the master's perspective, as well. If you oversaw these servants, you would not give them such significant amounts of money to steward if you did not believe they could handle it. If you had given that one talent to either of the other servants, it would have at least doubled in value. Instead, your trust in the third servant was completely wasted.

The third servant allowed his perception of his master to scare himself into inaction. He didn't even play it safe and invest it into the bank: he buried his talent because he was afraid.

Like the wicked servant, we can all too easily "bury" the gift of our singleness. For several struggling romantics I know, this fear looks like passivity. They live their lives with the desire to simply get through the day. They play hours upon hours of video games, stay in bed, and live with few—if any —commitments. They do the bare minimum to get through the day. For them, singleness is stagnancy: a period to do nothing and pursue nothing while they wait for the season to end. They live their lives as an endurance test rather than an invitation to something greater.

They put their lives on pause, their dreams on hold, until they find a spouse to share them with. They want to travel, but they don't want to travel alone. They have interests and opportunities they want to explore, but they wait to invest in those experiences until they find a spouse. They fear that if they fill their lives with other good things they're passionate about, they'll miss their person or won't have any room for a spouse in their lives. They don't realize that God has plans for them in the present moment. Instead, they bury their ambition for a future that may or may not come.

Then, there are struggling romantics who do nothing but pursue. They work hard, travel often, and go on lots of dates, but they don't make space for God to have a say in any of it. Church is nice, if they have time. Prayer is a life-line instead of a practice. Sabbath is out of the question. They are using their talents, but not for the master. In doing so, they end up missing the point entirely. They fear that if they slow down, loneliness and fatigue will catch up to them. Their busyness is a distraction from what matters most: their relationship with Jesus.

There's nothing inherently wrong with yearning to share experiences with your future spouse or wanting to pursue success. These things aren't bad on their own, they're bad when they come from fear. If we are to avoid burying our singleness in the ground, we need to live a life full of Christ and free of fear.

The time to seek God is now. The time to use your talents to serve him is now. The Bible warns us time is running out:

"the world is passing away along with its desires, but whoever does the will of God abides forever" (1 John 2:17).

When you stand before God and give an account for what you did with the talents he gave you, God isn't going to care about the video games you played or the position you held at your last job. He isn't going to count those moments you *thought* about doing something instead of actually doing it. He's going to count the moments you took the talents he gave you and did something with them. He's going to care about how you used them to bless others.

MULTIPLYING WHAT WE HAVE

If we are to live out our singleness in a manner that pleases God, we need to steward it well. In addition to the free time and flexibility singleness brings, we each have unique talents and skills we can use for God's glory.

I saw this in an unmarried woman I knew who deeply desired to have children. She expected to get married and then have biological children, but as years passed, she grew tired of waiting for an eligible man to arrive. So, she decided to adopt a child and become a single mother.

Another woman had a similar desire but a different response. She was close friends with a pastor and his young family and chose to invest in them, babysitting their kids so the pastor and his wife could spend time developing their relationship with each other. Both women stewarded their singleness to bless those around them.

I know some singles who have invited friends along on vacations that were originally intended for their future spouse. Because of the time together, those friendships deepened. Some single guys I'm close to have studied Greek and Hebrew in an effort to more fully appreciate the Bible.

God is inviting you to receive his love and contribute to its distribution. His love for you is not based on your performance: if it was, nothing you did would come close to earning it. We see this with the master in Jesus' parable. He is actually quite gracious: he accepts the servant who doubled five talents the same way he does the one who doubled two talents. He wasn't concerned with the *quantity* of talents, he was concerned about how his servants stewarded what was entrusted to them. What if you took a portion of the time you normally played video games or watched your favorite shows, and used it to do something meaningful instead?

The best ability you have in your singleness is your "yes". As a single, you have more ways to use your time, gifts, and income to love others than anyone else in any other life stage is able to. Perhaps a married couple just moved into the neighborhood, or there's another single who doesn't have any plans for the holidays, or there's a desire you have to start a small group at your church. The world, the church, and the marrieds need godly singles, just as we need them, in turn.

RUNNING THE RACE

Singleness and marriage are both marathons. I've never heard anyone boast about winning first place in a marathon, but they boast about having finished it. They trained for that moment and pushed themselves through to the end. It didn't matter how fast or how slow, the point is that they stayed in the race and finished.

You don't become a great husband or a great wife by getting married. You also can't live the single life faithfully just by being single. It takes training, patience, and a dedication to stay in the race. It isn't about being the perfect couple or the perfect single—it's about finishing the race well.

In what many consider the last book Paul ever wrote before his death, he writes about this as he reflects on his life.

> I have fought the good fight, I have finished the race, I have kept the faith. Henceforth there is laid up for me the crown of righteousness, which the Lord, the righteous judge, will award to me on that day, and not only to me but also to all who have loved his appearing.

(2 Timothy 4:7-8)

I am still running the marathon of singleness. When I am face-to-face with Christ, I want to tell him I stewarded my singleness well. Should God bless me with marriage, I want to be able to tell him I stewarded my marriage well. In either case, my finish line remains the same. God doesn't care how fast I'm running. What he cares about is that I'm staying on the path he's set before me. The point isn't about *how* I'm running; it's about *where* I'm running.

I have remained single longer than I thought I would, and for no lack of trying, either. There are times when it has felt burdensome and empty. But God has done things in me and through me that could not have happened or would not translate the same if I'd been married. The singles groups that I led would not have existed. This book wouldn't exist, either.

I don't believe my desire for a spouse will ever go away. But God isn't calling me to extinguish my desire; he's calling me to trust him with it. Under him, all desires are put in their proper contexts and given their fullest expression. If I do not get married in this life, I will experience an eternal marriage with Christ that will make a human spouse look like a pet rock in comparison. In God, I can't lose.

Whether I'm single or married, God's work in me will never be finished. There will always be new facets of his love to explore and new aspects of my own brokenness to address.

I leave you with this, dear reader: the God of the universe loves you. He wants you. He doesn't promise a pain-free life, but he does promise a purposeful one. So long as you walk with Christ, everything you go through will be worth it in the end.

The question isn't if God has plans for your life, it's whether or not you choose to follow them. He has invited you to play a part in his plan for the world. He doesn't mind your baggage, your history, your mistakes, or your present struggles. His hand is outstretched. All you have to do is say "yes".

Put your running shoes on. It's time.

Reflection Questions:

• Have you ever said "no" to something and later regretted it? Have you ever said "yes" to something that you didn't feel prepared for? How did those responses work out for you?

• How can you bless others in your singleness? What skills or passions can you uniquely offer your church and your community?

• Imagine a memoir was written about your life. What do you wish it would say about your single years?

LITURGY FOR THE STRUGGLING ROMANTIC

For moments when the yearning seems too much. To be spoken as a prayer, when all other words feel insufficient.

I come to you, O Christ,
in great need of your comfort.
The deepest foundations of
my soul ache and I cry out to you,
for a familiar longing has once again
pierced my innermost being.

I suffer under a love that has been aroused
despite its time not having arrived.
Longings have been stirred
for intimacy, for marriage, for children,
for a future that I do not have and fear I never will.
My whole being screams for relief
as if afflicted by an itch no hand can scratch.

Holy Spirit, intercede now on my behalf
for my soul groans in ways
which words fail to fully express.

SINGLENESS FOR STRUGGLING ROMANTICS

In the midst of my agitation,
straighten the paths of my mind
and calm the waters of my heart.

Creator God, see me in my anguish
for I bear the mark of your relational likeness.
See the body you crafted, which trembles with desire
as a raging fire that burns
without water to quench its flames.
See the mind you sculpted, which relentlessly moves
as a roaring tempest
spinning in violent and endless circles.

Wonderful Counselor, hold me close
as the father of the prodigal son
who ran to him and would not let him go.
Embrace me as a shepherd would
the lamb he searched so tirelessly to find.
Bring warmth to me and touch my heart.
Do not leave me to languish alone
or abandon me in my moment of need.

Jesus Christ, one who took on flesh
and faced the same struggles and temptations,
tend to me now in mine.
As your death tore the veil in the temple
so that nothing would remain between us,
bring to my mind the intimacy
which you pursue and freely offer me.

O Jealous God, the Original Romantic,
the one who zealously yearns for me,
who joined Isaac to Rebekah and Ruth to Boaz,
and, after joining Adam and Eve in the garden,
declared that your work was "very good",
see that I lie in my own garden alone.
Join me to one with a heart like yours
one whom you desire for me
and yet, regardless,
not my will, but yours be done.

Gracious Friend, comfort my aching heart
and to its longings, give an answer.
Let my weary bones enter your rest.
Establish my steps and show me the way I should go,
for your thoughts are precious to me.
While my plans may fail, you have established
a time and a season for everything.
If this is a time to delight in love,
then bless the cries of my heart
and lead me to the one you have prepared.
If this is a time to wait a little longer,
then direct my thoughts to focus on you
and let love awaken in the appointed season.
If this is a time that will last for the rest of my days,
then sanctify my body, that it may glorify you,
and bring to my mind the eternity we will share.
Who am I, O God, that you would listen to me?
What have I done, that you would seek me?
I will remind myself of your goodness

and rejoice, for you have never forsaken me.
I thirst for you and delight in your ways,
for in you my soul is replenished.
I give to you my burdens and fix my eyes on you.
You sustain me, and I will bless your name
when you give and when you take away.
In your peace, I will hope beyond my present agony
and face the day with renewed strength,
for I know your plans will not delay.

I am yours.
Amen.[1]

APPENDIX II

ON SEXUAL SINS

Paul warns his protégé, Timothy, "the time is coming when people will not endure sound teaching, but having itching ears they will accumulate for themselves teachers to suit their own passions, and will turn away from listening to the truth and wander off into myths" (2 Tim. 4:3-4). This has become especially true for our culture today in the realm of sexuality.

When it comes to reconciling our faith with our sexuality, there have been attempts to cut corners and justify "freeing" our sexual desires in spite of the truths in scripture. We see "problems" with the biblical sexual ethic and invent "fixes" for these perceived issues. But these are all false solutions to our desire for intimacy. Each assumes something about marriage that is, ultimately, incorrect. In so doing, it "corrects" a problem that never existed in the first place.

Many of these are controversial: most topics dealing with sex are. But we tend to base appropriate sexual expression on what *we* permit, instead of what *God* permits, and this needs to change. When we consider sex as the language of marriage, and marriage as a reflection of Christ and the church, discerning these issues becomes far more straightforward.

PORNOGRAPHY

This is a well-known problem, both in the church and outside of it. However, because pornography is so accessible and so prevalent, we can justify watching it as no big deal. What's the harm if everyone else is doing it?

We rationalize what we watch as harmless. The Bible, however, doesn't agree. Jesus says that "everyone who looks at a woman with lustful intent has already committed adultery with her in his heart. If your right eye causes you to sin, tear it out and throw it away. For it is better that you lose one of your members than that your whole body be thrown into hell" (Matt. 5:27-29). What we watch has consequences.

Porn can become an unintended instruction manual, a source of sexual education in the wake of silence from parents and churches. Its effects, especially on adolescents, are well-documented: exposure to pornographic images generally increases sexual thoughts, casual sexual behavior, sexual dissatisfaction, sexual uncertainty, as well as sexual aggression in boys and sexual victimization in girls.[1] This can happen well before puberty: one study found that some men were first exposed to porn as young as five years old.[2] How we see other men or women invariably affects how we treat them.

Pornography twists our expectations for sex, often at the expense of women. Females become objects to obtain, and sex becomes a source for selfish pursuit instead of a selfless sacrificial love. Because sex acts are easier to witness, the sacredness of sex is diminished. Pornography is far from harmless.

MASTURBATION

This is an elephant in the room that many Christian circles, at least the ones I've participated in, rarely address directly or say by name. Masturbation is a difficult struggle because it is powered by imagination and fantasy. For this reason, it is often complemented by pornography, though it can persist without it.

Fundamentally, masturbation is a form of sex outside of marriage. Lauren Winner articulates the harm masturbation poses.

> Masturbation teaches us that immediate gratification is a part of sex, and masturbation removes sex from a relationship. Indeed, the whole point of masturbation is to provide the release and pleasure of orgasm without the work and joy of a relationship.[3]

Masturbation decouples people from sex and makes sex *only* about meeting your own needs. It offers the physical feelings of sex, with none of the commitment or intimacy.

The Bible is incredibly pro-sex, sometimes in ways that would make you blush. It urges men to "rejoice in the wife of your youth, a lovely deer, a graceful doe. Let her breasts fill you at all times with delight; be intoxicated always in her love" (Prov. 5:18-19). Masturbation targets the delight found in sex and isolates it, detaching it from relationship.

It also amplifies loneliness. The hormones activated during orgasm attach themselves to fantasies and fictitious scenarios that disappear after the pleasure is gone. You attach yourself to nothing. If sexual intercourse is an amplifier, then masturbation only ends up amplifying loneliness.

COHABITATION

This is our primary modern solution to the "problem" of marriage. Marriage requires commitment, a willingness to endure hardship, and sacrificial love. Cohabitation removes both commitment and sacrificial love and replaces them with a relationship that either partner can abandon at any time, despite the financial, material, and emotional stakes that living together entails. More people are cohabitating now than ever before. At present, more American adults have cohabitated than have been married.[4] It's seen as a next step before marriage, a way to save on expenses, and a "test drive" of compatibility.

Contrary to what many of us might assume, most couples don't actually decide to live together. The majority of cohabiting couples slide into it, spending so many nights with each other that living together informally begins to happen.[5]

Cohabitation is an area that western churches have largely failed to confront, which is especially concerning as elements of cohabitation are making their way into Christian relationships. Many couples will hang out alone in each other's living spaces indiscriminately, and spend most of their time together in private instead of public places. I call it "fauxhabitation."

Despite the perceived benefits, cohabitation (in all of its forms) is decidedly *not* the ideal alternative or precursor to marriage that people hope it is. Compared to married couples, cohabiting couples have lower levels of trust and satisfaction.[6] For both men and women, cohabitation also doubles the chance of separation.[7]

Part of why cohabitation is so destructive is that it bases your relationship on performance instead of sacrificial love. Because there is nothing legally or spiritually binding them together, both partners need to consistently meet each other's needs in order to keep the relationship alive. Essentially, you need to keep your partner emotionally, mentally, and sexually satisfied, otherwise the relationship will be over. If your partner fails to live up to your desires, and you meet someone else that appears to, what is keeping you in the relationship? Breaking up is far messier, with shared possessions and assets (and sometimes children) needing to be divided between the two partners.

If marriage serves as a reflection of Christ and the Church, it shouldn't be based on performance. If a relationship exists for individual gain, then it cannot be sacrificial. When Christ sacrificed himself to the cross and offered us eternal life, he did so without conditions. If he had, we would be screwed! We can never please him or always make him happy, yet, in spite of that, he sacrificed himself for us. Our faith isn't based on performance, and marriage isn't, either.

SAME-SEX RELATIONSHIPS & POLYAMORY

In recent years, the conversation about faith and sexuality has broadened to include all manner of attractions and sexual preferences. We look at Adam and Eve, asking ourselves if, perhaps, there can be an Adam and Steve, or Adam and Steve and Eve. But Genesis makes it clear that "a man shall leave his father and his mother and hold fast to his wife" (Gen. 2:24). Marriage is designed to be one man and one woman in an exclusive sexual relationship ("one flesh") for the rest of their lives. Jesus reaffirms this same verse later on (Matt. 19:4-5).

Polyamory—having multiple partners at once—is becoming more accepted in our culture. And yet, as followers of Jesus, this isn't acceptable for us. Marriage reflects God's relationship with the church, and God is not an adulterous god (Ex. 20:3). Jesus reinforces that we are to love God with *all* of who we are (Matt. 22:37-38), not part of who we are. If God wants an exclusive relationship with us and no one else, then we are to do the same in our marriages.

Scripture is also clear that homosexual relationships of any kind, be it marital or romantic, are contrary to God (Rom. 1:26-27). Having said that, many churches have not been careful in regard to addressing this topic and have treated same-sex attraction (feelings for people of the same gender) and same-sex relationships with the same severity.

There are many people I know who wrestle with same-sex desires. We can't control the feeling of attraction, only what we do with it once we feel it. Someone with same-sex attraction, or SSA, can involuntarily feel drawn to someone of the same gender, but that, in and of itself, is not a sin. We need to remember that Jesus, as a perfect man, felt temptation (Heb. 4:15). Feeling temptation is not a sin if we don't give in to it. As someone with heterosexual desires, there have been married women I have felt attraction to. These desires aren't sin *per se,* but they can readily lead to it. You can't necessarily control attraction, but you can control your response to it.

Jesse is a single man who struggles with SSA. The moment he discovered his attraction toward other men, Jesse was hesitant to share it with anyone. His closest friend had a brother with a similar struggle who decided to tell his parents about it one day—they promptly kicked him out of the house. Stories like these taught Jesse his desires would be better kept to himself.

That all changed one night, in a prayer room in college, when Jesse finally opened up about his struggle to a friend of his. He was afraid they would reject him after he shared, but their reaction caught him off guard.

> The guy's response was to just look at me and say, "Hey, I still love you and God still loves you." He didn't drill me with theology. I don't think we really even unpacked it much more after that, but just his response of being with me in that moment as I just, you know, confessed the most vulnerable thing I've ever confessed . . . I think it was *the* most reassuring thing.[8]

That encounter cemented the fact that while same-sex attraction was a part of Jesse's life, it didn't define his entire identity.

Not everyone has Jesse's story. There are many individuals with the same temptations and a lack of safe avenues to ask questions. For other people with SSA, even contexts such as accountability groups can be dicey. Meeting Christians of the same gender who struggle with same-sex attraction can risk amplifying the temptations instead of conquering them. Then, there's the stigma people have in associating homosexuality with pedophilia and other sexual perversions. While this association isn't true, it gives people who struggle with SSA—especially those in ministry positions—another reason to avoid opening up.

But, as Jesse's story shows, the solution is love within a safe community. Vulnerability is a major part of love: without it, we cannot be seen and known fully by others. As Jesse looks back on that night, he said, "The reactions from the first people I told really set the trajectory for my life, like straight up . . . I opened up to them, and they met me with grace, and didn't see me any other way."9

DIVORCE

While divorce is probably not on the mind of most young singles, it needs to be included because many people find themselves single again due to divorce. Plus, other singles, ones who haven't experienced divorce, can seek marriage with the mindset that divorce is an optional exit in case of emergencies. In reality, divorce is a messy, ugly, and deeply painful process. Of husbands and wives, Jesus says, "they are no longer two but one flesh. What therefore God has joined together, let not man separate" (Matt 19:6). Marriage isn't merely a social institution, but a spiritual one. It isn't merely a priest or wedding officiant who marries the couple, but God himself.

Divorce is devastating, and it comes with extensive collateral damage. It affects families, especially children and in-laws. It affects the couple's mutual friends as well as the church they attend. But divorce is particularly destructive to children of the married couple, especially younger children. I saw this with a girl I worked with, whose parents had divorced. Her life was spent bouncing between four different homes: her mom's, her mom's parents, her dad's, and her dad's parents. In order to keep track of her things, she kept her entire wardrobe in her car. Summing up life after the divorce, she remarked, "My parents may be happier, but I'm not."

Despite the firm biblical warning against it, there are concessions. Divorce is permitted in the event of sexual immorality (Matt. 5:32, 19:9) and if an unbelieving spouse abandons the marriage (1 Cor. 7:15). There are also compelling arguments made about divorce due to abuse in the marriage. But—and this cannot be stressed enough—these concessions are exceptions to the rule. Marriage was not made to be broken.

There is much to unpack about divorce that cannot be covered here. Instead, I want to hone in on our approach and attitude toward divorce. As struggling romantics, we must not pursue marriage under the assumption that "if it doesn't work out, I can always get a divorce." Divorce isn't an escape hatch—it's a sad reality of our broken world. It's an undesirable last resort, if it should even be considered at all.

APPENDIX III

THE ABCs OF PREPARING FOR MARRIAGE

"Preparing for marriage" is a concept that seems more clear-cut for engaged couples than it does for struggling romantics. If you're engaged, you can go to premarital counseling or have conversations with your pastor, families, and married friends. If you're a struggling romantic, the path to marriage can feel vague and undefined.

Making a list of what to look for in your future spouse is great—having standards is good and necessary. But if we're not careful, we can add more and more expectations or raise the standards we have to an unattainable level. We can end up committing ourselves to a list instead of a person. With this list[1], my hope is that you will be equipped with practical steps to consider as you live as a single. Remember: this is not a substitute for scripture. It's a starting point for the practically-minded. Besides, the Word of God is vastly superior to that of a paltry coffee-drinker. Following instructions out of obligation is a road to legalism, not freedom.

Some may take issue with the phrasing "preparing for marriage", insisting that no one can ever be fully prepared for marriage. That might be true. However, it *is* possible to be fully *unprepared* for marriage. Surely, we can remedy that.

Let's be less unprepared for marriage, together:

A – ATTEND church regularly. Get your butt out of your chair and go in-person, once a week. This may feel a bit basic, but the basics of our faith are what matter most. If you aren't actively connecting with a local church, then you aren't actively connecting with the Body of Christ. Some people try making a case against going because churches are full of flawed and imperfect people. Guess what? You're flawed and imperfect, too. You'll fit right in.

B – Establish BOUNDARIES in your relationships. In your dating life and your friendships with the opposite gender, know where the physical and emotional lines are. If it helps, write down the traits you want in a future spouse: both the optional attributes, as well as the dealbreakers. Healthy boundaries aren't killjoys, they're safeguards. If someone doesn't respect your boundaries or feigns ignorance of them, double down and distance yourself from them if it gets bad enough. I have yet to meet singles or couples who regretted having too many boundaries in place. Often, it's the opposite.

C – Find spiritual COMMUNITY. Seek people who speak wisdom into your life and know you on a deeper level. Join a small group. Even if you're not socially wired, find at least one meaningful friendship, someone who sharpens you just as you sharpen them, a person who imitates Christ well. Keep persevering in your pursuit of people: deep friendships take time and can't be rushed. These should be people with whom you can safely share your heart and your relationship with Jesus.

D – Bring your DESIRES to God. Whenever we feel a deep yearning—whether for sex, marriage, children, or a partner—we have a temptation to take that desire and withdraw from God. Find a way to articulate these feelings, whether through prayer or talking to someone you trust. If you process better by journaling, write letters to God about your future spouse. These practices reinforce God as the center of your life and build trust in him.

E – ENJOY what you have. Look at your life and thank God for what he's already given you. It could be something specific, like hanging out with friends, or something obvious like being able to breathe. When you find reasons to be contented, you open your eyes to what God has already blessed you with. Find peace with what you already have, and you'll be less anxious with what you don't.

F – Keep your primary FOCUS on Jesus. Instead of centering your life around career success or finding a spouse or making enough to pay the bills, we must "seek first the kingdom of God and his righteousness, and all these things will be added to you" (Matt. 6:33). Before you add someone else to your life, be sure you have your own house in order. Are you seeking God above everything else? Are you giving him a say in how you spend your money? Who you date? Where you spend your time? When something else replaces

Jesus as our number one love, he won't force himself back into that position. It's on us to routinely reestablish Jesus on the throne of our lives.

G – Pursue GUIDANCE from people who are further ahead in their faith than you are. You can find wise counsel in mentors, other singles, and married couples: people both inside and outside of your season of life who further enrich your relationship with Jesus. Online influencers can offer insight, but they don't know you on a personal (much less spiritual) level. Make an in-person connection. Find a safe person of the same gender to hold you accountable in areas of temptation and sin.

H – HUMBLE yourself. Although Jesus was fully God, he took the form of a servant, even washing his disciples' feet. "If I then, your Lord and Teacher, have washed your feet, you also ought to wash one another's feet. For I have given you an example, that you also should do just as I have done to you" (John 13:14-15). As sinners, we don't deserve a spouse or a happy life: the only thing we deserve is hell. But Jesus freely gave his own life in place of ours so we could avoid the death we deserve. Anything in addition to that is a testament to the graciousness of God. One of the most dangerous prayers you could ever ask is for God to humble you. Pray it. I dare you.

I – Live a life of INTEGRITY. If you value Christ above all else, your life will look different than other people's. As believers, our faith is reflected by the habits and choices we make every day. If you believe that men or women should be treated with dignity, then that should affect the way you date them or how you talk about them when they're not around. Be consistent with how you live your life. Don't just talk the talk, take the step toward walking the walk.

J – Watch how you JOKE. "Let there be no filthiness nor foolish talk nor crude joking, which are out of place, but instead let there be thanksgiving" (Eph. 5:4). Sexual innuendos reinforce a malformed view of sexuality. Likewise, slandering former exes or negatively generalizing the opposite gender exposes a heart of unforgiveness. Our casual commentary has substantial impact on the lives of others, and it starts with the heart. The words we say, including our humor, should uplift and honor the other. We must ensure our language comes from a redeemed place of love and not a broken place of hurt.

K – KNOW more about what you believe and why you believe it. Theology doesn't replace having a relationship with God, but when it's added to our faith, it brings clarity and depth to our understanding of God and scripture. Use your singleness as an opportunity to learn about God on a deeper level. If you think you already know all there is about God and faith, you don't know enough.

L – Extinguish LUST in your life. Many people do "spring cleaning" as an excuse to purge their homes of dirt, dust, and unused items. Use your faith, likewise, to do the same with lust. Paul is adamant that "sexual immorality and all impurity or covetousness must not even be named among you, as is proper among saints" (Eph. 5:3). Paul isn't saying "get perfect or get out": he's highlighting the standard of sanctity among the children of God. Find an accountability partner to confide in about your sexual brokenness, abstain from having sex outside of marriage, cease masturbating, avoid watching pornography, and eliminate any other destructive behaviors. You won't be perfect, but having tools to deal with your sexual baggage goes a long way. Work on yourself in this area, and you'll be shocked by what fruit it produces.

M – Carefully filter the MEDIA you consume. Movies, shows, podcasts, influencers, video games, social media, online dating . . . be conscious of how the content you're watching affects you. Our culture frowns on such restrictions, but if the content you consume perpetuates low self-esteem, lustful fantasies, or jealousy toward others, then it isn't bringing you closer to God. Check the content of a movie online before watching it. Delete social media, or sell your TV if you have to. Your digital diet doesn't have to be exclusively Christian-themed media, but what you consume should incline your heart and your mind to glorify God. What you watch doesn't go in one ear and out the other, it affects your perception of others.

N – Getting NAKED with someone is a no-no. I mentioned this earlier in the list, but it bears repeating. Sex in any form outside of marriage is contrary to God's design. Singles and couples alike often grapple with "how far is too far" regarding physical boundaries, but if you have to ask the question, you're already too far. You are dating a brother or a sister of Christ, so treat them like a brother or sister.

O – OBSERVE other couples and singles in your life. Third wheel. Spend time with married couples and families. Take notes on how they love and communicate with each other, how they include (or exclude) other people, and what the effects of those decisions are. See what's happening in the relationships around you through the lens of scripture. This isn't just helpful for your future marriage, this is helpful in seeing how to presently (and practically) love others. There's a lot to learn about relationships by simply watching.

P – PRAY for your enemies. If loving your enemy is difficult for you to do, prayer is an excellent place to start. Few of us might label someone an "enemy" in our life, but there are certainly people we wouldn't consider friends, either. If there is someone who hurt you that you harbor anger toward, including an ex, pray for them. Watch how you talk about them to others, including God. If there is a person you are deeply jealous of, ask God to provide for them. Pray for their spiritual flourishing instead of them spontaneously falling into a ravine.

Q – Learn to ask good QUESTIONS. It's amazing how powerful a thought-out question can be, not to mention the answers that can result from it. Learn to be curious, genuinely curious, about someone other than yourself. Find things about them that captivate you and lean into those, especially with those you disagree with. Listening well and asking good questions are skills that take time to learn but are powerful tools for intentional connection. If you're stuck on what to ask someone, try asking them a question you wish they had asked you.

R – Implement healthy RHYTHMS. The greatest changes to someone's life don't typically happen through dramatic events: they begin through small, daily habits. Establish spiritual disciplines of reading your Bible and praying every day. Listen to sermons. Try regular exercise. Learn to make food at home. Create a budget, and manage your finances wisely. Not only are these skills useful in your life, but they will be a blessing to your spouse if you need to call upon them in your married life.

S – Learn to embrace SILENCE. If God spoke to you in a whisper instead of in a storm, would you be able to hear it (1 Kings 19:12)? Use the solitary moments in your life to connect with God. Drive without listening to music. Do errands while leaving your phone in the car. This isn't so you can fall asleep; be alert and present with God. Listen to what he has to say. Mind you, there's a difference between being alone *from* God and being alone *with* God. In the Gospels, Jesus didn't withdraw from people because he was depressed or hated being around others, he withdrew to connect one-on-one with God (Mark 6:45-46, among other examples). The essence of holy silence isn't to be in conversation or to be clear-headed before communing with God: it's simply to *be*. Quiet your heart and make room to hear God's voice.

T – Sanctify your THOUGHTS. Most sin begins in your mind. The way we think tremendously influences how we perceive the world. We must "take every thought captive to obey Christ" (2 Cor. 10:5). Flee from lustful fantasies. Reject thoughts of bitterness, jealousy, and envy. It is hard to live as single when your mind dwells on being married. Instead, "whatever is true, whatever is honorable, whatever is just, whatever is pure, whatever is lovely, whatever is commendable, if there is any excellence, if there is anything worthy of praise, think about these things" (Phil. 4:8). Your thoughts inform your perspective, and your perspective informs your actions.

U – Lean into what is UNIQUE about you. God made you in a slightly different way than everyone else. You're weird. We all are. Do you find yourself occupied with third-world countries more than most people you know? Do you enjoy writing whenever you have some extra time? Do certain issues ignite a passion within you? Interesting. You should look into that more. Explore your weirdness and see where it takes you.

V – VOLUNTEER time to ministry. Serve somewhere you never have before or follow the aforementioned weirdness you have. Get involved in the Body of Christ. If you feel burned out, take a break. Stop serving. You heard me. Withdraw to spend time with God and get filled up. The kingdom of God isn't glorified by those who serve out of duty instead of love. We need you and we need your gifts, so steward yourself and your energy well.

W – Seek WISDOM from God. "If any of you lacks wisdom, let him ask God, who gives generously to all without reproach, and it will be given him" (James 1:5). Wisdom is the ability to properly apply God's Word to our daily lives. Spoiler alert: all of us need wisdom, especially those of us who think we're already wise. It's freely available from God! Asking for wisdom emphasizes our reliance on him. When I'm in a difficult conversation or about to make an important decision, I will silently pray for wisdom. After all, God's the one whose guidance is actually useful, not mine.

X – Put an X-RAY to your brain and heart. Not literally, of course. That would be expensive. Instead, we need to apply a mental and emotional X-ray to ourselves so that we can identify and seek healing for our wounds. We all have traumas, hurts, or shame that inform how we see others and ourselves. Without recognizing these scars for what they are, our pain is apt to come out in all kinds of unintended and harmful ways. Without the right tools to navigate the hurt, we either self-medicate in sin or suffer helplessly without knowing how to address it. By understanding ourselves more fully, we can better articulate our needs and shortcomings. Go to therapy. Talk with trusted mentors and friends. Introspect. Journal. When we take the steps toward improving our mental and emotional health, our spiritual health flourishes as well.

Y – Lean into your "YES". As a single, you have more freedom and flexibility than anyone else, and this allows you to serve and invest like no one else can. It could be volunteer opportunities, prayer meetings, mission trips, babysitting, small groups, road trips, and more. This isn't about saying "yes" to everything: you know yourself best. Saying "no" to something we don't have the capacity for can allow us to say "yes" to something that's a better fit. Get out of your comfort zone, and explore opportunities locally or globally. If you're tempted to say "no" out of fear, try saying "yes", and see what happens.

Z – Don't relationally ZIGZAG with other people. Communicate your intentions clearly and kindly. Don't couch your words in vague verbiage. If you're romantically interested in someone, don't say ambiguous things like, "You know, I really enjoy hanging out with you." If someone seems interested in you, but you aren't interested in them, don't flirt with them. If you're taking a break from dating, don't act like you're not. Subtlety has its place, but not when it replaces clarity. It implies, but never clarifies. Jesus says you should simply "let your 'Yes' be 'Yes,' and your 'No,' 'No'" (Matt. 5:37 NKJV). Don't waste someone's time with games: Be upfront in what you say, loving in how you say it, and true to those you say it to.

NOTES

Introduction

1. I want to apologize to all the Tiffanys out there for making a joke at your expense. It's nothing personal: I just thought it sounded funnier that way. This endnote apology has been dedicated to you.

Chapter 1: More Than a Label

1. Sam Allberry, *7 Myths about Singleness* (Crossway, 2019), 13. For a deeper dive on singleness, this book is an incredible resource.
2. Ibid., 36.
3. John Chapman, "The Holy Vocation of Singleness: The Single Person in the Family of God," *Journal for Biblical Manhood & Womanhood* 5, no. 2 (2000): 4-5, https://cbmw.org/wp-content/uploads/2013/05/5-2.pdf.
4. Timothy Keller, *The Meaning of Marriage* (Penguin Books, 2016), 238.

Chapter 2: The Biggest Lies Singles Believe

1. Barry, personal interview with author, transcript, January 24, 2024.

Chapter 3: Single...for Life?!

1. Lauren F. Winner, "Solitary Refinement," *Christianity Today*, June 11, 2001, accessed December 4, 2024, https://www.christianitytoday.com/2001/06/solitary-refinement/.

2. U.S. Census Bureau, U.S. Department of Commerce, "Median Age at First Marriage," 2023. *American Community Survey, ACS 5-Year Estimates Detailed Tables, Table B12007*, 2023, accessed on May 30, 2025, https://data.census.gov/table/ACSDT5Y2023.B12007?q=B12007:+Median+Age+at+First+Marriage.

3. U.S. Census Bureau, "Median Age at First Marriage," 2010. *American Community Survey, ACS 5-Year Estimates Detailed Tables, Table B12007*, 2010, accessed on May 30, 2025, https://data.census.gov/table/ACSDT5Y2010.B12007?q=B12007:+Median+Age+at+First+Marriage.

4. Rebeca, personal interview with author, transcript, May 26, 2023.

5. Ibid.

Chapter 4: Marriage Mania

1. Marshall Segal, *Not Yet Married: The Pursuit of Joy in Singleness and Dating* (Crossway, 2017), 24.

2. John Chapman, "The Holy Vocation of Singleness: The Single Person in the Family of God," *Journal for Biblical Manhood & Womanhood* 5, no. 2 (2000): 4-5, https://cbmw.org/wp-content/uploads/2013/05/5-2.pdf.

3. Rebeca, personal interview with author, transcript, May 26, 2023.
4. Nancy Wilson, *Why Isn't a Pretty Girl Like You Married? and Other Useful Comments* (Canon Press, 2010), 12.
5. Segal, *Not Yet Married*, 96.

Chapter 5: Falling for a Caricature

1. Annibale Carracci, quoted in E.H. Gombrich and Ernst Kris, *Caricature* (Penguin Books, 1940), 11-12.
2. Randy Alcorn, *Heaven* (Tyndale House Publishers, 2004), 350.

Chapter 6: Writing Your Love Story

1. Vivian Tejada, "Strengthening Structures: Tips for an Earthquake-proof House," *Point*, August 19, 2024, accessed November 6, 2024, https://point.com/blog/tips-for-an-earthquake-proof-house.
2. Mike Cosper, host, *The Rise and Fall of Mars Hill*, episode 2, "Boomers, The Big Sort, and Really, Really Big Churches," June 28, 2021, accessed November 6, 2024, https://www.christianitytoday.com/podcasts/the-rise-and-fall-of-mars-hill/mars-hill-podcast-boomers-big-sort-hybels-warren-driscoll/.

Chapter 7: The Comparison Game

1. Arlene Pellicane, "When Your Marriage Doesn't Measure Up," *Christianity Today*, May 2, 2016, accessed December 11, 2024, https://

www.christianitytoday.com/2016/05/when-my-marriage-doesnt-measure-up/.

2. Nate Hilgenkamp, "Comparison | 7 Deadly Sins of Suburbia," Harris Creek Baptist Church, uploaded February 7, 2022, accessed December 13, 2024, YouTube video, 12:29, https://youtu.be/6JGOJdE06t4?si=LO5SPgBYgJkCNSxI. I was already considering many of the ideas for this chapter when I came across this sermon online.

Chapter 8: How to Be Attractive

1. Caroline, Karin Kratina, and Hannah Allen, "Aquaman and Abs: Hollywood's Unrealistic Body Standards Now Focused on Male Actors," *Dr. Karin Kratina & Dr. Hannah Allen: Nutrition Therapy*, accessed December 17, 2024, https://eatingwisdom.com/blog/aquaman-and-abs-hollywoods-unrealistic-body-standards-for-men.

2. Jocelyn Gecker, "Damage More Than Skin Deep: Young Girls Are Using Anti-Aging Products They See on Social Media," *Daily Herald*, September 8, 2024, accessed December 17, 2024, https://www.dailyherald.com/20240906/health-and-fitness/damage-more-than-skin-deep-young-girls-are-using-anti-aging-products-they-see-on-social-media/.

3. Matt Lantz, "Is It Possible to Make Yourself More Attractive?" *A Method for Dating*, May 29, 2011, https://thedatingblook.wordpress.com/2011/05/29/chapter1-2/.

Chapter 9: Taming the Workhorse

1. Peter Scazzero, *Emotionally Healthy Spirituality* (Zondervan, 2014), 100.
2. Jefferson Bethke, *To Hell With the Hustle: Reclaiming Your Life in an Overworked, Overspent, and Overconnected World* (Thomas Nelson, 2019), 179.

Chapter 10: Friends Wanted

1. Gallup and Meta, *The Global State of Social Connections*, 2023, Accessed December 18, 2024, https://www.gallup.com/file/analytics/513347/ Gallup-Meta-Global State of Social Connections Report-2023.pdf, 26.
2. "WHO Launches Commission to Foster Social Connection," *World Health Organization*, November 15, 2023, accessed October 8, 2024, www.who.int/ news/item/15-11-2023-who-launches-commission-to-foster-social-connection.
3. Derek Thompson, "Why Americans Suddenly Stopped Hanging Out," *The Atlantic*, February 14, 2024, accessed May 31, 2024, https:// www.theatlantic.com/ideas/archive/2024/02/ america-decline-hanging-out/677451/.
4. C.S. Lewis, *The Four Loves* (HarperOne, 2017), 114.
5. Stephen R. Covey, *The 7 Habits of Highly Effective People* (Simon & Schuster, 2020), 49.
6. Timothy Keller, "Marriage as Friendship," *Gospel in Life*, September 15, 1991, uploaded July 23, 2024, accessed November 14, 2024, https://

marriage.gospelinlife.com/e/marriage-as-friendship/.

7. Trevor Noah, "Simon Sinek & Trevor Noah on Friendship, Loneliness, Vulnerability, and More," Simon Sinek, uploaded September 9, 2024, accessed December 20, 2024, *YouTube* video, 22:09, https://youtu.be/CNBxIhxHHxM?si=SInHkJvxGx9ZfpDS.

8. *BoJack Horseman*, season 2, episode 10, "Yes And," directed by J.C. Gonzalez, written by Raphael Bob-Waksberg and Mehar Sethi, *Netflix* video, 26:06, aired July 17, 2015, https://www.netflix.com/watch/80048085.

9. Nancy Wilson, *Why Isn't a Pretty Girl Like You Married? and Other Useful Comments* (Canon Press, 2010), 91.

10. My fun spin on the original line, "You do not rise to the level of your goals. You fall to the level of your systems." by James Clear, *Atomic Habits: An Easy & Proven Way to Build Good Habits & Break Bad Ones* (Avery, 2018), 27.

Chapter 11: Seductive Fantasies

1. A. Guttmann, "Time Spent per Day With Major Media in the United States From 2019 to 2026," Statista, December 3, 2024, accessed June 19, 2025, https://www.statista.com/statistics/278544/time-spent-with-media-in-the-us/.

2. Conan O'Brien, "Conan's Full Q&A At The Oxford Union," Team Coco, uploaded March 5, 2020, accessed December 13, 2024, *YouTube* video, 18:19,

https://youtu.be/nMouIB-L8Nc?
si=H8VVmjS2h0xdD3nG.

3. "Tangled Directors' Hot Man Meetings," *Belfast Telegraph*, January 27, 2011, www.belfasttelegraph.co.uk/entertainment/film-tv/news/tangled-directors-hot-man-meetings/28584728.html.

4. Megan, personal interview with author, transcript, May 7, 2024.

5. Jamie Ballard, "Do Americans Believe in the Idea of Soulmates?," *YouGov*, February 10, 2021, today.yougov.com/society/articles/34094-soulmates-poll-survey-data.

6. Katie Bishop, "Why People Still Believe in the 'Soulmate Myth'," *BBC*, February 14, 2022, https://www.bbc.com/worklife/article/20220204-why-people-still-believe-in-the-soulmate-myth.

Chapter 12: Worshipping with Our Bodies

1. David Foster Wallace, "This is Water" (speech, Gambier, OH, May 21, 2005), Farnam Street, https://fs.blog/david-foster-wallace-this-is-water/.

2. John Kim, *Single on Purpose: Redefine Everything, Find Yourself First* (HarperCollins, 2021), 148.

3. Mark Regnerus, *The Future of Christian Marriage* (Oxford University Press, 2020), 92-93.

4. Jeff Diamant, "Half of U.S. Christians Say Casual Sex between Consenting Adults Is Sometimes or Always Acceptable," *Pew Research Center*, August 31, 2020, www.pewresearch.org/short-reads/2020/08/31/

half-of-u-s-christians-say-casual-sex-between-consenting-adults-is-sometimes-or-always-acceptable/.

5. "How are the Hormones Released During Sex like Human Super Glue?" *Options Health*, November 8, 2017, accessed December 11, 2024, https://optionshealth.org/blog/2017/how-are-the-hormones-released-during-sex-like-human-super-glue/.

6. Kat Harris, host, *The Refined Collective Podcast*, episode 126, "That's What He Said: Where Are All the Single Godly Men? With Ben Stuart," November 17, 2020, https://podcasts.apple.com/us/podcast/the-refined-collective-podcast/id1348034641?i=1000499104197.

7. John Kim, *Single on Purpose*, 148.

8. G.K. Chesterton, *Orthodoxy* (Doubleday, 1959), 95, quoted in Paul Brand and Philip Yancey, *Fearfully and Wonderfully Made* (Zondervan, 1980), 101.

Chapter 13: Emotional Horniness

1. If this topic resonates with you, I would highly recommend reading the final chapter of Sam Allberry's book *7 Myths about Singleness*.

2. C.S. Lewis, *The Screwtape Letters* (Scribner Paper Fiction, 1982), 36.

3. Margaret Clarkson, "Singleness: His Share for Me," *Christianity Today* 23, no. 10 (February 16, 1979): 15. https://www.christianitytoday.com/1979/02/

singleness-his-share-for-me-god-is-sufficient/.
Accessed November 13, 2024.

4. Barry, personal interview with author, transcript, January 24, 2024.

5. Paul Brand and Philip Yancey, *Fearfully and Wonderfully Made* (Zondervan, 1980), 154.

Chapter 14: To Date or Not to Date

1. Amanda Barroso, "Key Takeaways on Americans' Views of and Experiences with Dating and Relationships," *Pew Research Center,* August 20, 2020, www.pewresearch.org/short-reads/2020/08/20/key-takeaways-on-americans-views-of-and-experiences-with-dating-and-relationships/.

2. Tim Challies, "Lots of Single Christians but Few Weddings," February 5, 2025, accessed June 11, 2025, https://www.challies.com/articles/lots-of-single-christians-but-few-weddings/.

3. Kait Tomlin, host, *Heart of Dating*, "HOD SELECT: How to Drop the Hanky," 4:00, May 1, 2024, accessed December 13, 2024, https://podcasts.apple.com/us/podcast/heart-of-dating/id1358733969?i=1000654147285.

Chapter 15: Nine Ways to Become Irresistible

1. Ben Stuart. *Single. Dating. Engaged. Married.: Navigating Life and Love in the Modern Age* (W Publishing, 2017), 88.

2. Marshall Segal, *Not Yet Married: The Pursuit of Joy in Singleness and Dating* (Crossway, 2017), 93.

3. Gary Chapman, *The 5 Love Languages: The Secret to Love That Lasts* (Northfield Publishing, 2015), 138.

4. Annie F. Downs, host, *That Sounds Fun with Annie F. Downs*, "Summer Lovin': Dating 101 with Ben Stuart," June 1, 2023, accessed February 2, 2024, https://podcasts.apple.com/us/podcast/that-sounds-fun-with-annie-f-downs/id944925529?i=1000615259720.

5. Nancy Wilson, *Why Isn't a Pretty Girl Like You Married? and Other Useful Comments* (Canon Press, 2010), 83.

Appx. I: Liturgy for the Struggling Romantic

1. Verses for further reference: 2 Cor. 1:3-4; Ps. 130:1-2; Song 2:7; Lam. 3:55-57; Rom. 8:26-27; Prov. 3:5-6; Ps. 23:1-3; Ps. 34:18; Gen. 1:27; Eph. 2:10; Ps. 139; Matt. 8:23-27; Is. 9:6; Luke 15:1-10,20-24; Ps. 38:21; Heb. 4:15; Matt. 27:50-51; 1 Cor. 6:17; Ex. 34:14; James 4:5; Gen. 24:50-51; Ruth 4:13; Gen. 2:18-23; Luke 22:42-43; Ps. 37:23; Ps. 32:8; Ps. 139:17; Prov. 19:21; Ecc. 3:1; Ps. 63:1; Ps. 119:15; Ps. 27:14; Hab. 2:3.

Appx. II: On Sexual Sins

1. Jochen Peter and Patti M. Valkenburg, "Adolescents and Pornography: A Review of 20 Years of Research," *The Journal of Sex Research* 53, no. 4-5 (2016): 509–31. doi:10.1080/00224499.2016.1143441.

2. "Age of First Exposure to Pornography Shapes Men's Attitudes Toward Women," *American Psychological*

Association, August 3, 2017, accessed December 10, 2024, https://www.apa.org/news/press/releases/2017/08/pornography-exposure.

3. Lauren F. Winner, *Real Sex: The Naked Truth About Chastity* (Brazos, 2005), 113.

4. Juliana Menasce Horowitz, Nikki Graf, and Gretchen Livingston, "Marriage and Cohabitation in the U.S.," *Pew Research Center*, November 6, 2019, accessed December 10, 2024, https://www.pewresearch.org/social-trends/2019/11/06/marriage-and-cohabitation-in-the-u-s/.

5. Scott M. Stanley and Galena K. Rhoades, "What's the Plan? Cohabitation, Engagement, and Divorce," *Institute for Family Studies*, April 2023, accessed December 10, 2024, https://ifstudies.org/ifs-admin/resources/reports/cohabitationreportapr2023-final.pdf.

6. Horowitz et al., "Marriage and Cohabitation."

7. Mark Regnerus, *Cheap Sex: The Transformation of Men, Marriage, and Monogamy* (Oxford University Press, 2017), 164.

8. Jesse, personal interview with author, transcript, January 29, 2024.

9. Ibid.

Appx. III: The ABCs of Preparing for Marriage

1. This list was inspired by chapter 15 of *How to Stay Married: The Most Insane Love Story Ever Told* by Harrison Scott Key.

ACKNOWLEDGEMENTS

No book—at least, no *good* book—can be done alone. I am grateful to Mara Eller and Nancy Swanson for their indispensable editorial help. A special thanks to the four people I interviewed: Jesse, Barry, Megan, and Rebeca. I deeply appreciate each and every one of you for trusting me with your stories and allowing me to add them into this book.

I also want to thank the group of friends and family members—marrieds and singles alike—who provided feedback on my manuscript before it was published. A special shout-out goes to James and Sarah Newton, who offered valuable insight when the manuscript was still in its early stages. I would also like to thank Lem Dees, Jana Vastbinder, and Hannah Koch, who greatly supported me by reading and rereading the manuscript again and again. The significance of their feedback is dwarfed only by their friendship, which was essential in finishing this book: without them, I would still be rewriting my manuscript, second-guessing the material and wondering if it was any good.

There are others whose influence over this book was indirect yet important. Since this is my first-ever book, I am especially grateful for Sarah E. Westfall, a fellow author, who helped me with her advice and connections in the world of writing. A huge thank-you (though not huge enough) goes to my parents, David and Darlene Carpenter, for being continuous sources of wisdom and love in my life.

There are two men whose teachings greatly impacted my singleness, and consequently inspired much of this book: Ben Stuart and his book *Single. Dating. Engaged. Married.*, which greatly impacted my teenage years with its practical and comprehensive overview of faith in the world of romance; and Sam Allberry, whose book *7 Myths about Singleness* brought a deeper clarity and language to the beauty (and the struggle) I face as a single.

Finally, I want to thank everyone who has encouraged me along the way: your words gave me strength at times where I felt I had none to give. A special thanks goes out to the singles groups that I led in California and Indiana: I couldn't help but think of your faces as I wrote these chapters. I hope my words prove helpful to you and bring you (as well as everyone else reading this) into greater intimacy with Christ.

ABOUT THE AUTHOR

Daniel Carpenter is a starving artist who grew up in the northwest suburbs of Chicago and was educated at Huntington University. A storyteller at heart, Daniel spends his free time convincing innocent passersby that his opinions about movies and food are correct. Daniel can be found haunting various coffee shops, working on his next creative idea.

How has this book impacted you?
I would love to hear your story.

Send me an email at danielcarpentercreative@gmail.com.
Responses are not guaranteed, but appreciation is.